IDIOMS for Everyday Use

Milada Broukal

Illustrations by
Luques Nisset

National Textbook Company
a division of NTC/CONTEMPORARY PUBLISHING GROUP
Lincolnwood, Illinois USA

ISBN: 0-8442-0748-9

Published by National Textbook Company,
a division of NTC/Contemporary Publishing Group, Inc.,
4255 West Touhy Avenue,
Lincolnwood (Chicago), Illinois 60712-1975 U.S.A.
©1994 by NTC/Contemporary Publishing Group, Inc.

0 1 2 3 VL 18 17 16 15 14 13 12 11

Contents

U N I T   1

Idioms from Colors

Reading

Read the story. Then discuss the questions.

In the Red

The letter came **out of the blue**! I wasn't expecting it. But there it was **in black and white,** signed by the bank manager. I had no money in my checking account. I was **in the red.**

I couldn't believe it. So I went to see the manager. We looked at the problem together. The bank had made a mistake. It had put ten dollars into my account instead of one thousand dollars!

Because it was the bank's mistake, there was no delay reopening my account. The manager cut through all the **red tape.** Now I had money in my account. And I had **the green light** to write checks again.

1. Does **in the red** mean to have enough money or to not have enough money? When a company is in the red, is it in trouble?

2. When you learn something **out of the blue,** is it a surprise?

3. If doing something takes a lot of **red tape,** is it easy to do? Sometimes getting papers from the government takes a lot of red tape. Can you think of some examples of things that take red tape?

Meanings

Each example has an idiom with a color word. Read the example carefully to find the meaning of the idiom. Then look at the definitions that follow the examples. Write the idiom next to its definition.

the black market   You can go to the bank to change dollars. But if you change money on **the black market,** you often get more money for each dollar.

to feel blue   I was alone on my birthday and **feeling blue.** Then Anny called and invited me out, and I felt better.

the green light   The bank has given us the money. Now we have **the green light** to start the project.

green with envy   I was **green with envy** when I learned that Luis had won a trip to Europe.

in black and white   I couldn't believe it, but there it was **in black and white,** as clear as it could be. The letter said that I had won a trip to Europe.

in the black   Theo earns a thousand dollars a week. He doesn't have to worry about having enough money. He's always **in the black.**

in the red   I never have enough money to pay my bills. I'm always **in the red.**

out of the blue   The news of the factory's closing came **out of the blue.** No one was expecting it.

the red carpet   When the movie star visited, our town rolled out **the red carpet.** There was a parade and a special dinner in her honor.

red tape   Every time you want to get a new passport, you have to go through a lot of **red tape.** It's not easy and it takes a lot of time.

a white lie   I didn't feel like going out. So I told **a white lie,** and I said I didn't feel well.

1. _____ by surprise, unexpectedly

2. _____ very clear and easy to understand

3. _____ owing money, in debt

4. _____ complicated official procedures and forms

5. _____ the okay to start something

6. _____ special honors for a special or important person

7. _____ the market not controlled by the government, where things are sold in private and often against the law

8. _____ something that is not true but that causes no harm

9. _____ jealous of someone else's good fortune

10. _____ to feel sad

11. _____ having money

Practice

A. Answer each question with **yes** or **no.** Explain your answer.

1. My boss just gave me a raise in salary. Am I feeling blue?

2. I took my driver's test and passed. Then in less than half an hour I had my driver's license in my hand. Was there a lot of red tape?

3. My friend Jack asked if I liked his new purple tie. I didn't really like it, but I said that the tie was nice. Did I tell a white lie?

4. I always like to keep some extra money in the bank for an emergency. Am I in the black?

5. My boss said he had to talk to two other managers about my project. Did I get the green light?

6. They said it was in the contract, but I never saw it. Was the contract in black and white?

7. If I write this check, I won't have enough money in my account to cover it. Will I be in the red?

8. We had no idea at all. He told us he was leaving the company. Was the news out of the blue?

9. When the famous general came to town last year, we even had a special parade and fireworks show. Did the town roll out the red carpet?

10. When I exchange foreign currency at the bank, do I get it on the black market?

11. Sam wanted the job as manager of the store, but another employee got it. Might Sam be green with envy?

B. Each example has the correct idiom, but there is one error with each idiom. Find the error and correct it.

1. I got the news from the blue.

2. The rules for the contest were in black or white.

3. They were green for envy when their friend won the lottery.

4. Tony loves to shop, so he is always on the red.

5. You must go through a lot of red tapes to get a visa in some countries.

6. They rolled out the red carpets when he came.

7. Yuri does not have a problem with money. He's in black.

8. Pam was feeling in blue because she had to stay home.

9. I told white lie. I said I couldn't come to the party because I had other plans.

10. The city has the green lights to build a new highway.

11. The tourists bought some money on the black.

Conversation

Practice each conversation with a partner.

SITUATION 1

Tom is talking to his friend.

TOM: I just got a call from my brother.

CAROL: How is he?

TOM: Out of the blue he told me he just got married.

SITUATION 2

Jenny is feeling lonely.

LUCIA: You don't look very happy, Jenny.

JENNY: I'm just feeling blue. I guess I feel lonely.

LUCIA: Don't feel lonely. I'm your friend! That's why I came to take you out.

SITUATION 3

Nancy is talking to her husband.

NANCY: Let's go to a nice restaurant for supper.

MATT: Is there something special to celebrate?

NANCY: No, but I just finished doing our expenses for the month, and we're in the black. Let's spend some of our extra money.

On Your Own

Work with a partner. Choose three idioms. Write a short conversation for each idiom. Then act out your conversations.

Discussion

Work with a partner or in a small group. Do the following activities.

1. The idioms in this unit all use color words. What other idioms with color words in English do you know?

2. Are there idioms with colors in your native language? Are any idioms like the ones in English?

3. We use **out of the blue** when something unexpected happens. Tell a story using this idiom.

UNIT 2
Idioms from Food

Reading

Read the story. Then discuss the questions.

A Real Lemon

The used car I bought for three hundred dollars was **a lemon.** My friends said I was **nuts** to believe the **baloney** the seller gave. The seller said that the car was like new, with only ten thousand miles on it. She called it reliable transportation at a very low price. She said she was really selling it for **peanuts.**

Starting the engine of the car was **a piece of cake.** I just turned the key—no problem. However, soon I was **in a pickle:** the brakes didn't work! The owner of the Cadillac I hit **went bananas** when he saw the damage to the front of his car. He started shouting at me and wouldn't stop. Now I have to pay him two thousand dollars to repair his car. But my friend Nina was **a peach.** She took my car to the garbage dump so that I didn't have to see it again.

1. Does something that is **a lemon** work well? Have you ever bought a lemon?

2. Is something that is **a piece of cake** easy to do or hard to do? Name some things that are a piece of cake for you to do.

3. When someone **goes bananas,** what happens to the person?

Meanings

Each example has an idiom with a food word. Read the example carefully to find the meaning of the idiom. Then look at the definitions that follow the examples. Write the idiom next to its definition.

the apple of one's eye The baby is **the apple of her grandfather's eye.** He thinks that she's wonderful.

baloney His speech about the importance of helping the poor is **baloney.** He wouldn't even give his best friend a dime.

to cream someone Our basketball team really **creamed** its opponent. Our team won by a score of 120 to 60.

fishy On our return home, we found the front door open, and we suspected that something **fishy** was going on.

to go bananas She **went bananas** when she heard she had won first prize in the talent contest.

in a pickle Bill was **in a pickle.** After filling his car with gas, he could not find the money to pay.

a lemon The new tape player I bought was **a lemon,** and I'm going to take it back to the store for a new one.

nuts Tony must be **nuts** to pay over a hundred dollars for a shirt.

a peach When I was sick last week, Susan visited me and bought groceries for me. She's **a peach.**

peanuts Rose buys used clothes at secondhand stores, and she gets nice-looking clothes for **peanuts.**

a piece of cake The math test was **a piece of cake** for Erik. He is very good at doing math problems.

1. _____ in trouble

2. _____ something that is very easy to do

3. _____ something that does not work, usually an electrical appliance or mechanical item

4. _____ to totally beat someone in a game

5. _____ a very small amount of money

6. _____ nonsense

7. _____ suspicious, not right or honest

8. _____ to go crazy

9. _____ very crazy, very upset

10. _____ a very nice person

11. _____ someone's favorite person

Practice

A. Answer each question with **yes** or **no.** Explain your answer.

1. When the president gave Lou her award, they shook hands, and the audience applauded politely. Did the audience go bananas?

2. Sokolovshy beat Splatski 11 to 1 in the chess championship. Did he cream Splatski?

3. Someone on the street offered to sell me a gold watch for five dollars. Was something fishy happening?

4. When dad was making breakfast, the bacon caught on fire. Was making breakfast a piece of cake for him?

5. My car has only three thousand miles on it and has already been to the garage five times for repairs. Is it a lemon?

6. The salesperson told me he could give a big discount, just for me. Was he probably talking baloney?

7. John has a good job and today he won a million dollars in the lottery. Is he in a pickle?

8. John just gave a million dollars to a stranger. Will people say that he's nuts?

9. Maria went to a fancy store and paid full price for her furniture. Did she buy the furniture for peanuts?

10. Bob Kent thinks his daughter is the best. Is she the apple of his eye?

11. Karen promised to spend Saturday helping me cook the food for the party. Is Karen a peach?

B. Each example has the correct idiom, but there is one error with each idiom. Find the error and correct it.

1. Using the computer was so easy, it was piece of cake.

2. Something fish must be happening. We're the only ones here, but I'm hearing strange noises.

3. That man doesn't know anything, but he talks as if he knows everything. Everything he says is the baloney.

4. My new TV is lemon. It has a very bad picture.

5. Millie was in pickle when the police officer stopped her for speeding.

6. The dog went nut when its owner came home.

7. In the soccer tournament, our team crammed its opponent 8 to 1.

8. The team went banana when it won the championship.

9. Norma is very nice. She's peach.

10. Jason bought a used stereo for a peanut, and it sounds really good.

11. I'm the apple of my grandmother's eyes.

Conversation

Practice each conversation with a partner.

SITUATION 1

Maria is talking to her neighbor.

MARIA: I'm in a pickle. I'm having a big party, and I don't have enough glasses or dishes.

KATE: Don't worry. I'll lend you some of mine.

MARIA: Thanks, Kate. You're a peach!

SITUATION 2

Tran is talking to his friend Ho about the basketball game.

TRAN: We won the game 110 to 58 last night.

HO: You guys really creamed the other team.

TRAN: We sure did.

SITUATION 3

Theo and Helen have just taken a test.

THEO: That test was so easy!

HELEN: Yes, it was a piece of cake. I'm sure I passed.

On Your Own

Work with a partner. Choose three idioms. Write a short conversation for each idiom. Then act out your conversations.

Discussion

Work with a partner or in a small group. Do the following activities.

1. The idioms in this unit all use words related to food. Do you know any other idioms in English that use food words?

2. Are there idioms with food words in your native language? Are any of those idioms like the ones in English?

3. **To be in a pickle** means to be in trouble. Tell about a situation in which you were in a pickle.

Idioms from Numbers

Reading

Read the story. Then discuss the questions.

To Go Fishing, or Not to Go Fishing

For some people, fishing is so enjoyable that it puts them **in seventh heaven.** For others, fishing is a good time to relax and catch **forty winks.** I'm **of two minds** about it. **At first sight,** fishing seems like fun. But, **on second thought,** I just don't like to handle a fish when I catch it. To many people who like fishing, it's **second nature** to look at a river or a lake and know where the fish are. They have a **sixth sense** that helps them do this. Soon they're catching fish, while I'm still trying to put the worm on the hook.

1. When you are **in seventh heaven,** how do you feel?

2. When you are **of two minds,** have you made a decision? Name some things about which you are of two minds.

3. If doing something is **second nature** to you, is it easy or hard for you to do? Name something that is second nature to you.

Meanings

Each example has an idiom with a number. Read the example carefully to find the meaning of the idiom. Then look at the definitions that follow the examples. Write the idiom next to its definition. **Note:** You will use the same definition for two idioms.

at first sight   I don't know what to think about the new boss. **At first sight,** she seems okay, but I may change my mind later.

forty winks   I sometimes take **forty winks** on Saturday afternoon, so that I can continue working around the house afterward.

in seventh heaven   Maxwell was **in seventh heaven** when he learned he had gotten the job.

of two minds   Betty was **of two minds** about her future: Should she study to be a teacher or an actress?

on cloud nine   Juanita was **on cloud nine** when she graduated from college at the top of her class.

on second thought   You know that large-screen TV I was going to buy? **On second thought,** I decided to keep my old TV for a while.

to put two and two together   We saw our neighbors putting suitcases into their car. So we **put two and two together** and concluded that they were going away on a trip.

second nature   Learning to golf is **second nature** to some people. They can hit the ball well with no problem the very first time.

second to none   The food in that restaurant is **second to none.** You really get the best meals there.

six of one, half a dozen of the other   We can either stay home or go to the movie. I don't care. For me, it's **six of one, half a dozen of the other.**

sixth sense   Lisa has a **sixth sense** for directions. She always knows which road to take to get where she wants to go.

1. _____   a short sleep, a nap

2. _____   changing one's mind after thinking more about something

3. _____   extremely happy

   _____

4. _____   a special feeling for something, or a special understanding of things

5. _____   easy and natural to someone

6. _____   no difference, either choice okay

_____

7. _____   having trouble making a decision

8. _____   to finally understand something, to come to a conclusion about something

_____

9. _____   the very best

10. _____   after a quick look, before really thinking about one's feeling about something

Practice

A. Answer each question with **yes** or **no.** Explain your answer.

1. We saw several people kneeling on the ground and touching it. We guessed that they were looking for a lost contact lens. Did we put two and two together?

2. I just had forty winks. Did I sleep all night?

3. Sal's hamburgers are the best in the world. Are they second to none?

4. If you never change your mind, can you say that you're always of two minds?

5. Richard got a speeding ticket. Was he in seventh heaven?

6. Marilyn won the lottery. Was she on cloud nine?

7. I don't care whether we go to the beach or to the park. Is it six of one, half a dozen of the other?

8. When I first looked at my English homework, I thought that it would take a half hour. But I spent two hours on the homework. Was I right at first sight?

9. Aretha had never ridden a horse before, but she got on one and rode away. Was riding second nature to her?

10. Jason wanted that sport jacket, but now he isn't sure. Is he having second thoughts?

11. Mike knew it was me when I phoned him. Does he have a sixth sense?

MY SIXTH SENSE TELLS ME THAT YOU WON'T CATCH ANYTHING TODAY.

B. Complete each example with an idiom from this unit. (For one example, you can use two idioms.)

1. _____, I thought the price was a bargain, but now I'm not so sure.

2. Arthur never needed piano lessons. For him, playing was just _____.

3. American jeans are the best in the world. They're _____.

4. Hiroshi is _____ about whether he wants to continue school or get a job.

5. _____, I've changed my mind, and I don't want the extra cheese on my burger.

6. Bert finally _____. He had forgotten to plug in the computer.

7. Avril has been _____ since she passed her exams.

8. Lin needed a short rest, so she took _____.

9. My _____ tells me that it's going to rain and that I'll need my umbrella today.

10. For me, it's _____. We can go either for Chinese food or for Italian food.

Conversation

Practice each conversation with a partner.

SITUATION 1

A customer is thinking about buying a car.

WILL: This model is second to none. It's nice-looking and reliable, and it gets good mileage.

KEN: Oh, really?

WILL: That's right. It's our best-selling model.

SITUATION 2

The conversation continues.

WILL: So what do you think of the car?

KEN: I don't know. I'm of two minds about it. I think I need something bigger.

WILL: No problem. Just think about it.

SITUATION 3

The customer comes back another day.

WILL: So, are you still thinking about the car?

KEN: On second thought, I need a station wagon.

WILL: Well, do I have a deal for you! We're selling this model over here at a very good price.

On Your Own

Work with a partner. Choose three idioms. Write a short conversation for each idiom. Then act out your conversations.

Discussion

Work with a partner or in a small group. Do the following activities.

1. The idioms in this unit all use numbers. Do you know any other English idioms that use numbers?

2. Are there idioms with numbers in your native language? Are any idioms like the ones in English?

3. Would you be **on cloud nine** if your **sixth sense** told you that the captain of the airplane in which you were flying was taking **forty winks**? Describe why or why not.

4. When were you last **in seventh heaven**? Describe what happened.

Idioms from Parts of the Body

Reading

Read the story. Then discuss the questions.

What a Group!

Last year my English class was full of characters. That's a polite way of saying it had some unusual people that I'll never forget. One student was such a hard worker that he learned all the idioms in our book **by heart.** He was always saying things like "I'm on cloud nine," or "I'm green with envy." We never knew if he meant what he said or if he was just practicing English. Another student **had a sweet tooth.** She would bake lots of breads and cakes and bring them to every class for us to share during breaks. Two students met in the class and fell **head over heels in love.** We were all invited to their wedding and had a great time. Then there was a student who was always **pulling someone's leg.** For example, one day before class, he put a long homework assignment on the board and made us think that the teacher had given it. We all had **long faces** until the teacher came in. Then we realized that someone had played a joke on us.

1. What do you do when you learn things **by heart**? Tell about some things that you have learned by heart.

2. When someone **pulls your leg,** is the person telling the truth? Is the person always being mean?

3. How do you feel when you have **a long face**? If you have a long face, are you showing your feelings?

Meanings

Each example has an idiom with a part or parts of the body. Read the example carefully to find the meaning of the idiom. Then look at the definitions that follow the examples. Write the idiom next to its definition.

a big mouth	My brother has such **a big mouth.** He told everything I said to our mother.
by heart	I know all my friends' telephone numbers **by heart.** I never have to look in the telephone book.
to cost an arm and a leg	Everything in that fancy department store **costs an arm and a leg.** I can't afford to buy anything there, not even a pencil.
to have a sweet tooth	I know you **have a sweet tooth,** so I bought you a box of chocolates.
head over heels in love	Pam and Tony are **head over heels in love.** They're planning to get married.
a long face	Because Judy didn't get an invitation to the party, she's walked around with **a long face** since yesterday.
nosey	Every time I go out, I notice my **nosey** neighbors watching me. They must know everything about me.
a pain in the neck	Waiting for the bus on the cold, windy corner is **a pain in the neck.**
to pull someone's leg	Tomorrow is not a holiday. Don't believe Rich. He's just **pulling your leg.**
to see eye to eye	Lucy and Dick never argue. They **see eye to eye** on almost everything.
to shake a leg	**Shake a leg**! We have to be at school in twenty minutes.

1. _____ to like sweet foods very much

2. _____ always wanting to know other people's business and what other people are doing

3. _____ a person who talks too much and does not keep secrets

4. _____ to agree completely

5. _____ a sad, dissatisfied expression

6. _____ by memory

7. _____ to hurry up, move faster

8. _____ to be very expensive
   _____

9. _____ very much in love
   _____

10. _____ to joke, to kid or trick someone

11. _____ something or someone that annoys or bothers a person

Practice

A. Answer each question with **yes** or **no.** Explain your answer.

1. Barbara and Bob are always fighting. Do they see eye to eye?

2. Alicia never says a word. Does she have a big mouth?

3. Our neighbor Christine keeps coming to our house for no reason. Is it possible that she's being nosey?

4. Sid loves to eat pickles, olives, and anything salty. Does he have a sweet tooth?

5. Joseph thinks Maggie is the most wonderful person in the world. All he thinks about is Maggie. Is he head over heels in love?

6. The only problem with this school is the parking. There are no spaces, and it takes an hour to find a spot. Is parking a pain in the neck?

7. I got this book in the sale. It was eighty percent off the original price and cost almost nothing. Did it cost an arm and a leg?

8. Yoko did not get the job she applied for. She looks very unhappy. Does she have a long face?

9. Walter told us it was his birthday, but it wasn't true. Was he pulling our leg?

10. I can count from one to ten in French, Italian, and Greek. Did I learn this by heart?

11. Derek hurried and had only a quick bite to eat because he wanted to get to the movie on time. Did he shake a leg?

B. Each example has the correct idiom, but there is one error with each idiom. Find the error and correct it.

1. George really had the long face because he had lost his wallet.

2. Our neighbors are noseys.

3. She loves cakes. She has such a sweet teeth.

4. They never see by eye.

5. That person has big mouth.

6. Come on! Shake legs!

7. Lisa is head on heels in love with Steve.

8. Driving in this terrible traffic is a pain my neck.

9. Don't believe her. She's pulling your legs.

10. I learned that poem by my heart.

11. That excellent stereo system must cost a leg and an arm.

Conversation

Practice each conversation with a partner.

SITUATION 1

Beth and Amy want to get Sandy a small gift for her birthday.

BETH: What should we get Sandy?

AMY: I know she has a sweet tooth.

BETH: That's easy then. We'll get her a box of chocolates.

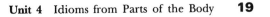

SITUATION 2

Chris needs to buy something at the store.

CHRIS: What time does the store close?

SUE: In twenty minutes.

CHRIS: Let's shake a leg then!

SITUATION 3

Two students are talking about their schoolwork.

PETE: I still haven't done the book report. When is it due?

LIN: Tomorrow.

PETE: Are you sure?

LIN: No. I was just pulling your leg. It's due next week.

On Your Own

Work with a partner. Choose three idioms. Write a short conversation for each idiom. Then act out your conversations.

Discussion

Work with a partner or in a small group. Do the following activities.

1. The idioms in this unit use words from parts of the body. Do you know any other English idioms with words from parts of the body?

2. Are there idioms in your native language that use words from parts of the body? Are any idioms like the ones in English?

3. What are the good and bad things about **having a sweet tooth**?

UNIT 5

Idioms from People

Reading

Read the story. Then discuss the questions.

The Real McCoy

Our boss Virgil is a very original person. He started a business from nothing, and now he's a millionaire. Although he is such **a man of means,** he remains a sincere, helpful person. If any of his friends needs help, he's the first to give it. He's a true friend, **the real McCoy.**

He does all sorts of jobs in his company, from typing out his own letters to repairing big machines. He's **a jack of all trades.** And he doesn't bother about **keeping up with the Joneses.** He doesn't care what people think of his life-style; he doesn't have to have a lot of expensive things. He still drives the old car that he bought ten years ago, and he sometimes wears jeans to work.

1. If someone is **a man or woman of means,** what does the person have a lot of?

2. What can **a jack of all trades** do?

3. If you want to **keep up with the Joneses,** what do you do?

Meanings

Each example has an idiom with people or a person's name. Read the example carefully to find the meaning of the idiom. Then look at the definitions that follow the examples. Write the idiom next to its definition. **Note:** You will use the same definition for two idioms.

to go Dutch

When I go out to eat with my friends, we usually **go Dutch.** This way everyone knows what he or she is spending.

a jack of all trades

Louise can fix TVs, paint houses, and build shelves. She's **a jack of all trades.**

to keep up with the Joneses

Kate and Ken just bought the same car as Mavis and Mick, the same drapes as Dinah and Dick, the same chihuahua as Antonio and Antonia. They're really **keeping up with the Joneses.**

a man/girl Friday

Griselda wants to get some work experience, and she likes to do a lot of different things. So she's gotten a job as **a girl Friday** at the local TV studio.

a man/woman of means

My cousin has a business that makes a large profit every year. He's **a man of means.**

the real McCoy

The large diamond in her ring isn't an imitation. It's **the real McCoy.**

to run in the family

Omar and his sister are both very thin. Being skinny must **run in the family.**

a smart aleck

Alexandra is such **a smart aleck.** She always thinks she's right about everything and always makes you think that you're wrong.

Tom, Dick, or Harry

The boss was very careful about whom he hired for the job, and he interviewed several people. He didn't just hire any **Tom, Dick, or Harry.**

a wise guy

Don't be such **a wise guy** and act as if you know it all. Other people won't like you.

1. _____   a true example of something

2. _____
_____   to want the same nice things that other people have

3. _____   a person who can do many things

4. _____   a rich person

5. _____   to share the cost, to pay one's own bill

6. _____
_____   someone who acts as if he or she knows everything and is often rude about it

7. _____   nobody special, just any person

8. _____   someone who does a large variety of tasks on the job

9. _____   to be characterized by something common to many members of a family

_____

Practice

A. Answer each question with **yes** or **no.** Explain your answer.

1. When the neighbors bought a Mercedes, Frieda told her husband they had to have one too. Is Frieda trying to keep up with the Joneses?

2. George always wears the same old pants and shirt, and he drives a broken-down old car. Does George look like a man of means?

3. Fabian spends a lot of time and money trying to look different from anyone else. Does he want to look like Tom, Dick, or Harry?

4. Kevin and Mary went out on a date, and Kevin paid for the meal and movie. Did they go Dutch?

5. Chung is always polite and is willing to listen to other people's opinions in discussions. Is Chung a wise guy?

6. Emma is a very good plumber, but she can't do painting or carpentry or other things around the house. Is Emma a jack of all trades?

7. Elaine's father and mother are doctors, and Elaine is studying to become one. Does being a doctor run in the family?

8. This wooden bed is a genuine antique. It's two hundred years old. Is it the real McCoy?

9. Mathilda's only job at the office is to answer the telephone. Is she a girl Friday?

10. When I suggested that we go to a restaurant for our class party, Liz said that I had made a stupid suggestion, as usual. Was Liz being a smart aleck?

B. Each example has the correct idiom, but there is one error with each idiom. Find the error and correct it.

1. This ring is real McCoy. It's genuine.

2. Bart is broke because he wants to keep up with the Jones.

3. The president of our company is a woman of mean.

4. What we need in this office is a girl on Friday.

5. Be careful with Ben. He's somewhat of wise guy.

6. Being good at math goes in my family.

7. I don't like to work with her. She's such smart aleck.

8. I don't lend my car to just any Tom, Dick, and Harry.

9. At last I found Andy the handyman. He's a jack in all trades.

10. Amanda asked Richard to go on a date, but she said that they would run Dutch.

Conversation

Practice each conversation with a partner.

SITUATION 1

Two friends are having a conversation.

MOSES: That's a beautiful watch!

LAURA: Thank you, Moses. I got it for my birthday.

MOSES: Is it a real Mucci?

LAURA: Oh yes, it's the real McCoy.

SITUATION 2

At the office, Rebecca is talking to her secretary, Janet.

JANET: Okay, the copier is running again.

REBECCA: I can't believe you fixed it! You're really a jack of all trades.

SITUATION 3

Two friends are talking about someone they know.

YUKO: Did you hear about Kathy?

PAM: Yes, I heard she's going to get married, but I don't know who he is.

YUKO: Well, he's a man of means, I can tell you that.

PAM: I guess we all know Kathy wouldn't marry just any Tom, Dick, or Harry.

YUKO: I wonder where she found him?

On Your Own

Work with a partner. Choose three idioms. Write a short conversation for each idiom. Then act out your conversations.

Discussion

Work with a partner or in a small group. Do the following activities.

1. Are there idioms in your native language with people or people's names? Are any idioms like the ones in English?

2. **The real McCoy** is a true example of something. Describe two things that are the true example of something and say where you can find them.

3. Some people like to **keep up with the Joneses** and want to have what their friends or neighbors have. Describe a situation and use **keeping up with the Joneses.**

U N I T   6

Idioms from Animals

Reading

Read the story. Then discuss the questions.

Two Very Different Brothers

At school, Randy was shy and **as quiet as a mouse.** He was also very clever. He had a twin brother, Jason. Jason loved football and had to **work like a dog** to make good grades. In school, Randy was the **bookworm.** He loved to read. But without his glasses he could not see. He was **as blind as a bat.** Jason **ate like a horse** and was two hundred pounds at age seventeen. Both of them were **early birds** and got out of bed at four every morning. Randy read and studied. Jason went training. Today, because they were **pigheaded** and did not give up, Jason is quarterback for the Glendale Geeks, and Randy is the owner of the team.

1. If you **work like a dog,** do you work hard or don't you work hard? When have you worked like a dog?

2. Are you **an early bird**? Tell why or why not.

3. If you are **pigheaded,** do you change easily?

Meanings

Each example has an idiom with an animal word. Read the example carefully to find the meaning of the idiom. Then look at the definitions that follow the examples. Write the idiom next to its definition.

as blind as a bat I'm **as blind as a bat** without my glasses.

as quiet as a mouse When the teacher walked into the room, each student was at his or her desk, reading a book, **as quiet as a mouse.**

a bookworm Howard reads twelve books a week. He's a real **bookworm.**

a copycat My little brother Marvin is **a copycat.** If I get black sneakers, he wants to have black sneakers, too.

chicken Richard is too **chicken** to try waterskiing.

an early bird Allan arrives at the office before everyone else. He's **an early bird.**

to eat like a horse Every time Jess goes walking in the mountains, he comes home with a big appetite, and he **eats like a horse.**

pigheaded Adam is so **pigheaded** that he never listens to anyone. He always does what he has decided.

to smell a rat I could **smell a rat.** Someone stopped me on the street and offered to sell me a gold watch for five dollars.

to talk turkey Let's stop being polite and talking around the problem. Let's start **to talk turkey.**

to work like a dog Javier works two jobs and goes to college. He **works like a dog** because he wants to get a good education.

1. _____ making almost no noise, being shy and not talking much

2. _____ to work very hard

3. _____ not taking advice, stubborn

4. _____ to eat a lot

5. _____ the first person to be somewhere, a person who gets out of bed early

6. _____ not able to see well because of very bad eyesight

7. _____ someone who reads a lot

8. _____ afraid, scared

9. _____ to talk openly and directly

10. _____ to think there may be something wrong

11. _____ a person who wants to do the same thing as other people

Practice

A. Answer each question with **yes** or **no.** Explain your answer.

1. Marvin stays in bed all day. Does he work like a dog?

2. Gloria always listens to other people's advice. Is she pigheaded?

3. Bert is very original. He dresses in his own style. Is he a copycat?

4. I can't see a thing without my glasses. Am I as blind as a bat?

5. Hank eats a lot. Does he eat like a horse?

6. Manuel never says very much. Is he as quiet as a mouse?

7. Carlo is always late. Is he an early bird?

8. If Stamo thinks there is something wrong or dishonest going on, does she smell a rat?

9. Are you chicken if you go skydiving?

10. If you won't talk openly to someone, will you talk turkey?

11. Larisa never reads. Is she a bookworm?

B. Complete each example with an idiom from this unit.

1. Janos goes to school all day and then works two evening jobs. He _____.

2. At the sale, the _____ will get all the bargains before anyone else arrives.

3. Andrew never speaks at meetings. He's

_____.

4. Reiko always wears the same clothes as her friends. She is such a _____.

5. Every time we invite Tony to dinner, he finishes every dish. He _____.

6. The store was advertising TVs for one hundred dollars. I _____.

7. Let's _____. We need to solve this problem quickly.

8. Jaime goes to the library three times a week because he's a _____.

9. You're just _____. Everyone can ride a bike.

10. Roger won't take advice from anyone. He's just plain _____.

11. I'm _____ without my glasses.

Conversation

Practice each conversation with a partner.

SITUATION 1

Alfred is asking Alice about her new neighbors.

ALFRED: What are your new neighbors like?

ALICE: I don't know. I haven't met them yet.

ALFRED: Oh, really.

ALICE: All I know is that I haven't heard a sound from next door. They're as quiet as mice.

SITUATION 2

Liza is talking to Nathan.

LIZA: Did you hear that Louis has a new girlfriend?

NATHAN: No, what's she like?

LIZA: I hear that she works in a library. Maybe she's a bit of a bookworm.

SITUATION 3

Kyle is talking to his little brother.

BRUCE: Can I ride on your bike?

KYLE: No, you can't. And stop being such a copycat. You don't have to do whatever I do.

BRUCE: Why not? What else are big brothers for?

On Your Own

Work with a partner. Choose three idioms. Write a short conversation for each idiom. Then act out your conversations.

Discussion

Work with a partner or in a small group. Do the following activities.

1. The idioms in this unit all use animals. Do you know any other English idioms that use animals?

2. Are there animal idioms in your native language? Are any idioms like the ones in English?

3. Would you **smell a rat** if someone who is normally **as quiet as a mouse** demanded that you **talk turkey**?

4. **A copycat** sees someone else do something and wants to do the same thing. Describe a situation where someone was a copycat.

U N I T   7

Idioms from Geography

Reading

Read the story. Then discuss the questions.

A Down-to-Earth-Town

Nothing much ever happens in our town. But, **once in a blue moon,** everyone gets excited about something. The town picnic in the ·middle of the summer is the big event of the year. People come to it from all over. But basically Bobtown is a quiet, sleepy old town. Some people say that it's **going downhill.** It is true that many citizens have moved away. There are empty houses, and real estate is **dirt cheap.** But the people who stayed have kept the spirit.

Yes, Bobtown is a simple place for simple people. People here are **down-to-earth.** They're not afraid to say what they think. They don't **make a mountain out of a molehill.** If a problem comes up, they solve it and don't waste time talking about how bad the situation is. Every election, the same mayor **wins by a landslide.** She gets all eighty votes.

1. If something happens **once in a blue moon,** does it happen often? Name something that you do once in a blue moon.

2. If something is **going downhill,** is it improving? Can you give an example of something you know that is going downhill?

3. If you **make a mountain out of a molehill,** what do you do?

Meanings

Each example has an idiom with a word from geography. Read the example carefully to find the meaning of the idiom. Then look at the definitions that follow the examples. Write the idiom next to its definition.

dirt cheap
She needed money badly. So she had a garage sale in which she sold a lot of her things **dirt cheap.**

down-to-earth
Oleg is always willing to give advice, and his advice is usually valuable. He's **down-to-earth.**

to go downhill
The company is **going downhill** rapidly. It needs to produce and sell more and better products.

to make a mountain out of a molehill
Sally usually gets good grades, but she didn't do well on the last test. Now she's very worried. I think she's **making a mountain out of a molehill.**

once in a blue moon
Katie is so busy that she sees her brother Kevin only **once in a blue moon.**

out of the woods
He was very ill, but he's getting better. He's **out of the woods.**

out of this world
The ice cream at that store is **out of this world.** I'd walk a mile to buy some.

over the hill
I used to be able to run five miles a day without any problem. Now I have trouble running just two miles. I must be getting **over the hill.**

the tip of the iceberg
Jonathan seems very unhappy. He says that he's having trouble in school, but I think that's only **the tip of the iceberg.**

up the creek
My car is in the repair shop again. Without it, I'm **up the creek** because I can't get to work.

to win by a landslide
Eighty-eight out of one hundred students chose Dan for class president. He **won by a landslide.**

1. _____   almost never, very seldom

2. _____   getting too old

3. _____   to get almost all of the votes
   _____

4. _____   honest and direct, sensible and practical

5. _____   very inexpensive

6. _____   out of the trouble or difficulty

7. _____   excellent, very good

8. _____   small part of a larger problem

   _____

9. _____   to make a big problem out of
                                          a small problem

   _____

   _____

10. _____   in trouble

11. _____   to go down in numbers or in quality, get
                                          worse

Practice

A. Answer each question with **yes** or **no.** Explain your answer.

1. Terry bought a secondhand car for almost nothing. Was the car dirt cheap?

2. The desserts at that restaurant are the best you've ever tasted. Are they out of this world?

3. Tony's legal problems as a result of the accident are still not over. He has to appear in court next week. Is he out of the woods?

4. You can count on Jan. She's honest and gives good advice. Is Jan a down-to-earth person?

5. We almost never go to the theater to see a play or a show, only for some grand occasion. Do we go to the theater once in a blue moon?

6. The soccer player is running more slowly and isn't as quick as he used to be. Is the player getting over the hill?

7. The president won the election by getting two percent more of the votes than the other candidate. Did the president win by a landslide?

8. Sally's tennis game is improving. Is her tennis game going downhill?

9. Stephanie burnt the chicken in the oven, but the way she described it, we all thought her kitchen burned down. Does Stephanie make a mountain out of a molehill?

10. Howie drove his friend's sports car and crashed it to pieces. The car was not insured and Howie doesn't even have a driver's license. Is Howie up the creek?

11. I have a lot of things to do. My English homework is just one small thing. Is the English homework just the tip of the iceberg?

B. Complete the idiom in each example with the correct word or words.

1. Fiona is a very down-_____-earth person. She's very sensible.

2. The pizza at this restaurant is _____ _____ this world.

3. Hans owes a lot of money. The money he owes me is _____ tip _____ _____ iceberg.

4. Esmerelda always makes _____ mountain _____ _____ _____ molehill.

5. The president won the election _____ _____ landslide.

6. We see her only once _____ _____ blue moon.

7. We're all happy to see him _____ _____ _____ woods.

8. We need to keep our neighborhood clean and in good repair. No one wants it _____ _____ downhill.

9. We bought this secondhand computer _____ cheap.

10. Ivan has real problems. He's really _____ _____ creek now.

11. Many athletes try to retire before they get over the _____.

Conversation

Practice each conversation with a partner.

SITUATION 1

Penny has come from out of town to visit Michelle. Michelle takes her to a local scenic spot.

MICHELLE: I come here only once in a blue moon now. What do you think of the view from here?

PENNY: It's out of this world.

SITUATION 2

Two people are talking about a recent election.

NICK: I didn't hear the news. Who won the election?

BRIAN: Bill Newton won by a landslide.

NICK: Well, I'm not surprised. The other candidate's ideas were a little over the hill.

SITUATION 3

Bud has a new stereo.

CHRIS: Did you get a new stereo?

BUD: Yes, I bought it dirt cheap.

CHRIS: How come?

BUD: The store was going out of business.

On Your Own

Work with a partner. Choose three idioms. Write a short conversation for each idiom. Then act out your conversations.

Discussion

Work with a partner or in a small group. Do the following activities.

1. Look over the list of idioms. Can you identify the word from geography in each one? What does each word mean?

2. Are there idioms in your native language that use words from geography? Are any idioms like the ones in English?

3. To be **up the creek** means to be in trouble. Describe a situation where you were up the creek.

4. Some people like to **make a mountain out of a molehill.** Tell a story using this idiom.

Idioms from Recreation

Reading

Read the story. Then discuss the questions.

A Person on the Ball

We always knew what our boss, Winona, was thinking. **Right off the bat,** as soon as she walked through the door, she'd let you know what she wanted you to do. Her style was clear, direct, and open. She always **put her cards on the table.**

If you did something wrong or said something inappropriate, Winona told you that you were **off base.** If she thought you were doing well and **on the ball,** she told you that, too. And when she said no, she meant no. **No dice.** Not many people argued with Winona and won. But I think she really enjoyed people who would stand up to her and give their own opinions. I think she secretly **got a kick out of it.**

1. **Right off the bat** is an idiom from baseball, in which a player hits a ball with a bat. If you do something right off the bat, when do you do it?

2. If you are **on the ball,** do you do things well?

3. If you **get a kick out of something,** do you enjoy it? What things do you get a kick out of?

Meanings

Each example has an idiom with a word from a recreation or sport. Read the example carefully to find the meaning of the idiom. Then look at the definitions that follow the examples. Write the idiom next to its definition.

to get a kick out of something　I really **get a kick out of** Lisa's jokes. She always makes me laugh.

to go fly a kite　I'm tired of listening to you complain. Stop bothering me. Why don't you just **go fly a kite**?

a good sport　I beat Albert five times at video games today, but he's such **a good sport** that he bought us a pizza afterward.

in the same boat　Now that we're both out of work, we're **in the same boat.**

to keep the ball rolling　Let's **keep the ball rolling.** We're off to a good start, but we still need to collect more money to get videotape machines for our school.

no dice　Tom wanted the party to be at my apartment, but I said **no dice.**

off base　You're **off base** with that answer. Try again.

on the ball　Sophie is an excellent manager. She really knows how to organize things and get things done. She is really **on the ball.**

to put one's cards on the table　**Let me put my cards on the table.** Either we sell more or we'll have to close the business.

right off the bat　Una looked at the math problem for just a minute, and she got the correct answer **right off the bat.**

sink or swim　We're going to do our best to start our own restaurant, **sink or swim.**

1. _____ very good at doing things, effective and efficient

2. _____ immediately, without delay

3. _____ to enjoy something a lot
   _____

4. _____ no, a negative answer

5. _____ someone who does not complain if he or she loses or who does not boast if he or she wins

6. _____   not to hide anything, to explain
   _____   the situation fully and honestly

7. _____   not correct, inappropriate

8. _____   in the same situation

9. _____   to make something continue to happen
   _____

10. _____   to go away or stop annoying someone,
                                        usually said in anger

11. _____   fail or succeed, no matter what

Practice

A. Answer each question with **yes** or **no.** Explain your answer.

1. Can we keep the ball rolling if everyone helps?

2. The bank said no dice about the loan. Is that good news?

3. Angel always complains when he loses at tennis. Is he a good sport?

4. If you tell someone to go fly a kite, are you being rude?

5. Are you off base if you give a really wrong answer?

6. Bernard seldom does a good job with anything. Is he on the ball?

7. If I wrote to you right off the bat, did I wait to do it?

8. If you put your cards on the table, do you hide anything?

9. If you get a kick out of something, do you enjoy it?

10. If we're in the same boat, do we have the same problem?

11. Dalia isn't the strongest runner, but she's training hard to make the track team. Is she determined to try to make the team, sink or swim?

B. Complete each example with an idiom from this unit.

1. We'll keep trying to find a way to solve the problem, but at the moment, I don't know if we'll

   _____.

2. Jack is a _____. He never gets upset when he loses.

3. Anthony is _____. He knows how to get things done well.

4. My father wouldn't lend us the money. He said _____.

5. I was so angry at Jimmy, I told him to _____.

6. Don't tell me you're having a hard time, too. We're _____.

7. To finish this job, we need to _____.

8. Some people really _____ watching football.

9. I started to work on the project, but I ran into a problem _____ and stopped.

10. I think that you're _____ by saying that sports are not useful or important.

11. I'm _____. There's no point in hesitating any longer.

Conversation

Practice each conversation with a partner.

SITUATION 1

Two people are discussing a problem.

HENRY: Stop complaining. We're all in the same boat.

MARY: But you told me to put my cards on the table.

HENRY: Yes, but complaining doesn't help.

SITUATION 2

The conversation continues.

MARY: Well, I think you were off base to tell me not to complain.

HENRY: Really? I was just saying what I think.

SITUATION 3

The conversation continues.

MARY: Do you get a kick out of arguing?

HENRY: I'm not the one who's arguing. You are.

MARY: Go fly a kite!

On Your Own

Work with a partner. Choose three idioms. Write a short conversation for each idiom. Then act out your conversations.

Discussion

Work with a partner or in a small group. Do the following activities.

1. The idioms in this unit all use words from recreation or sports. Do you know any other English idioms with words from recreation or sports?

2. Are there idioms that use words from recreation or sports in your native language? Are any idioms like the ones in English?

3. Look over the list of idioms. Some of them come from specific sports. For example, several come from baseball. Can you identify the idioms that come from specific sports? Which sports are they?

4. If you are never **on the ball** because your information is **off base,** do you think you'll **sink or swim**?

5. Some people do not complain if they win or lose. They're **good sports.** Describe a situation where someone was a good sport.

U N I T   9

Idioms with the Word *And*

Reading

Read the story. Then discuss the questions.

**Wear
and
Tear**

It's true that my car looks old and worn out. It's eleven years old, and it has a lot of **wear and tear** on it. But I'm tired of my friends telling me to get a new car. **By and large,** my car still runs okay. It takes me where I want to go. I use it to go **back and forth** to work every day, and it doesn't break down very often.

When it does break down, I take it to my mechanics. They know the **ins and outs** of my car. They don't give me **a song and dance.** They tell me exactly what's wrong with the car and how much it will cost to fix it. I know that I can trust them. So I feel confident that when I drive my car, it will get me **safe and sound** to where I'm going.

1. When something has a lot of **wear and tear,** how does it look?

2. To what places do you go **back and forth** often?

3. When you know the **ins and outs** of something, do you know it well? About what things do you know the ins and outs?

Meanings

Each example has an idiom with the word **and.** Read the example carefully to find the meaning of the idiom. Then look at the definitions that follow the examples. Write the idiom next to its definition.

back and forth
Elvis rode the same bus route for years. Every week he went **back and forth** from San Antonio to Austin.

by and large
By and large, Americans eat a light breakfast. They usually don't eat a lot of food in the morning.

a cock-and-bull story
George and I had a date for Saturday, but he never came to get me. Now he just told me **a cock-and-bull story** about thinking that our date was on Sunday.

fair and square
I won the checkers game **fair and square,** but Alex argued that I hadn't followed the rules.

ins and outs
If you know the **ins and outs** of computers, you should be able to get a good job.

odds and ends
I wanted to buy some clothes at the big sale, but by the time I got there, there were only **odds and ends** left.

right and left
We had a lot of business last week. The orders were coming in **right and left.**

safe and sound
I was worried when I first heard my brother had been in a car accident. But no one was hurt. Everyone was **safe and sound.**

a song and dance
I wish we didn't have to listen to such a long **song and dance** every time we want to get insurance.

spick-and-span
Calpurnia always cleans the house well before her mother visits so that everything is **spick-and-span.**

wear and tear
The carpet near the door gets a lot of **wear and tear** because we all walk on it as we come into the house.

1. _____ damage that happens as something gets old and used

2. _____ mostly, most often

3. _____ all the details

4. _____ a variety of small items, the pieces left over

5. _____ with no damage or injury

6. _____ a long explanation, a long excuse that is often not true

7. _____ an untrue story

8. _____ very clean

9. _____ from one place to another and back to the first place

10. _____ honestly, without cheating

11. _____ in large numbers, from every side

Practice

A. Answer each question with **yes** or **no**. Explain your answer.

1. Students who work hard usually succeed. Do students who work hard by and large succeed?

2. The witness told the truth, and everybody believed him. Was it a cock-and-bull story?

3. All Berta does is clean her house. It is so clean, you feel uncomfortable. Is her house spick-and-span?

4. When we opened the package, the vase was broken in a thousand pieces. Did the vase arrive safe and sound?

5. Every time I ask Ernest for the money he owes me, he tells me the many difficulties he is having with his job. Does Ernest go through a song and dance every time?

6. We got to the store on the last day of the sale. There was nothing special left to buy. Were there only odds and ends left?

7. We put an ad in the paper, but only one person called. Did we get calls from right and left?

8. Every weekday I go from my house to school, then back again. Do I go back and forth to school during the week?

9. The rug looked brand-new. I didn't even know it had been used. Did the rug show evidence of wear and tear?

10. Nassir has been working in that office for twenty-five years. He knows about everybody and everything in it. Does Nassir know the ins and outs of the office?

11. The referee makes sure that all the players follow the rules. Does the referee see that the game is played fair and square?

B. Each example has the correct idiom, but there is one error with each idiom. Find the error and correct it.

1. By or large, people put salt on their food.

2. With the odds and end she found in the garage, she made a chair.

3. No one likes to play with Peter because he doesn't play fair or square.

4. The kitchen was span-and-spick.

5. He always tells bull-and-cock stories.

6. She'll give you a song and dances as usual.

7. He goes from his bedroom to the kitchen, back and forward every morning, when he's getting ready for work.

8. I was really worried, but then they arrived safely and sound.

9. Ask Sandra. She knows all the in and outs.

10. These shoes can take a lot of wear and tore.

11. There were reporters all around the movie star. They were asking her questions right to left.

Conversation

Practice each conversation with a partner.

SITUATION 1

Terry is in a furniture store. She's looking for a sofa.

> TERRY: These sofas are nice, but I need one that can take a lot of wear and tear. You see, I have four children, two dogs, and a cat.

SALESPERSON: I have just the thing for you.

TERRY: That's not a bad-looking sofa.

SALESPERSON: And it's very strong and well made.

SITUATION 2

Ted and Bob are at work.

TED: Did Chuck hand in his work yet?

BOB: He called to give us the usual song and dance about how difficult it is to find people.

TED: I'm tired of always having to wait for his work.

SITUATION 3

Marta is talking about her new apartment.

PILAR: Is your apartment all ready?

MARTA: By and large, it is. I still have a few odds and ends to do.

PILAR: Can I help you with anything?

MARTA: Well, can you put up curtains?

On Your Own

Work with a partner. Choose three idioms. Write a short conversation for each idiom. Then act out your conversations.

Discussion

Work with a partner or in a small group. Do the following activities.

1. The idioms in this unit all use the word **and.** Do you know any other English idioms with **and**?

2. Are there idioms in your native language that use the word **and**? Are any idioms like the ones in English?

3. We use the idiom **safe and sound** when things or people are not harmed or hurt. Tell a story using this idiom.

Idioms from Household Items and Tools

Reading

Read the story. Then discuss the questions.

A Flash in the Pan

My friend Marta wanted me to be in the talent contest with her. I didn't want to get onstage. I have no talent. But she said that I was **a wet blanket** and that I never wanted to do anything fun. I decided **to throw in the towel** and not to argue with her.

At the contest, Marta sang a Beatles song. Then it was my turn. Fortunately, I'd found one of my nephew's old puppets. I did a ventriloquist act, in which it looked as if the puppet and I were trading old jokes. My friends who saw me onstage must have thought I **had a screw loose.** I was surprised that the audience laughed and seemed to enjoy my act. Then it was time for the winner of the contest to be named. I could see Marta, waiting **on pins and needles,** hoping to win. I could see that she was angry when my name was called. She didn't talk to me for a week. But now we've **buried the hatchet** and we are friends again. But my victory was **a flash in the pan.** I have never been onstage before or since.

1. Is **a wet blanket** a person who is fun to be with?

2. When you are **on pins and needles,** how do you feel? When are you on pins and needles?

3. When you **bury the hatchet,** do you make enemies with someone?

Meanings

Each example has an idiom with a household item or a tool. Read the example carefully to find the meaning of the idiom. Then look at the definitions that follow the examples. Write the idiom next to its definition.

as sharp as a tack   Tommy is only three, but he's **as sharp as a tack.** He can say the ABCs and can read some words.

to bury the hatchet   Let's forget our disagreement and **bury the hatchet.**

a flash in the pan   I got a 100 on the final test, but that was just **a flash in the pan.** I got low scores on all the rest of the tests, and I was barely able to pass the course.

to have a screw loose   Anatoly didn't take a jacket even though it was cold and windy. He must **have a screw loose.**

on pins and needles   I wasn't sure if I did well on the test. So I was **on pins and needles** when the teacher was giving them back.

to pan out   If things **pan out,** we hope to get a bank loan and start a computer service business.

potluck   Our end-of-class party was a **potluck** dinner for which each student made a special food.

soap opera   My aunt has watched the same **soap opera** on TV for ten years. She's very interested in all the difficult problems that the people in the soap opera have.

to sponge off   It's about time Gary got his own apartment. He's **sponged off** us long enough.

throw in the towel   When the candidate saw she couldn't win the election, she **threw in the towel** and quit the race.

a wet blanket   Andy is such **a wet blanket.** He never wants to go to parties, and if he does go, he won't dance.

1. _____   a person who doesn't enjoy things and keeps others from enjoying them

2. _____ to be crazy

3. _____ something that starts out well but that may not continue

4. _____ clever, intelligent

5. _____ to agree to no longer be enemies

6. _____ to succeed, to have a good result

7. _____ to take money or hospitality and never pay anything back

8. _____ a meal in which everybody brings a food to eat

9. _____ to accept defeat or loss

10. _____ a drama on TV or radio that continues over time and in which the characters have many problems

11. _____ very nervous and anxious

Practice

A. Answer each question with **yes** or **no.** Explain your answer.

1. We all had a great time at the picnic. Dorothy as usual complained about the food, how uncomfortable it was, and how many insects there were. Is Dorothy a wet blanket?

2. My wife prepared a special meal when my boss came over for dinner. Was it potluck?

3. Brian hoped to get the job as head teller in the bank, but he didn't get it. Did things pan out for Brian?

4. For years my best friend has been watching the story "Main Street" on television every afternoon. Does my friend like to watch soap operas?

5. Don thinks that creatures from other planets visit Earth all the time. Do you think Don has a screw loose?

6. Whenever Richard borrows anything from me, he immediately gives it back the next day. Does Richard sponge off me?

7. Jeff is always very calm before he has to take a test. Is he on pins and needles?

8. When I saw that I couldn't persuade them, I stopped arguing. Did I throw in the towel?

9. Every book this author writes is a success. The last one was a success too. Was it a flash in the pan?

I'M PUBLICLY ANNOUNCING THAT THIS IS MY LAST SHOW. I'M RETIRING FROM THE STAGE.

A FLASH IN THE PAN!

10. Brenda quarreled with her best friend, Judy, last week. But yesterday, they decided to be friends again. Did they bury the hatchet?

11. Lila is always well dressed when she goes to work. Is she as sharp as a tack?

B. Complete the idioms in each example with the correct word or words.

1. She's too lazy to work and sponges _____ her brother.

2. We won't invite him again. He's always _____ _____ blanket.

3. If I have enough money and things _____ _____, I'll take a trip this summer.

4. He sometimes talks to himself. I think he has _____ screw _____.

5. They just love to watch those _____ operas in the afternoon.

6. At the end of the close game, I was on _____ and _____, hoping our team would win.

7. At the meeting, no one paid attention to my arguments. So I threw in _____ _____.

8. His success today is only a flash _____ _____ pan.

9. After ten years of fighting, the two families decided to _____ _____ hatchet.

10. Ming can do this in no time. He's as sharp _____ _____ _____.

11. I brought a special salad to the _____ dinner.

Conversation

Practice each conversation with a partner.

SITUATION 1

Two friends are talking.

JOAN: Ted, what's wrong? You look so nervous.

TED: Yes, I'm on pins and needles, but nothing's wrong. I'm just waiting to hear if I got a bank loan.

JOAN: What are you planning to do with the money if you get it?

TED: If things pan out, I'm going to buy a house.

SITUATION 2

Another pair of friends is talking.

MARTHA: I want to be at home at one this afternoon to watch my soap opera.

ANNIE: Are you watching "Main Street"?

MARTHA: Yes. Today Buddy's finally going to bury the hatchet with his son. I just can't miss that!

SITUATION 3

A final pair of friends is talking.

KEN: What are your two nephews doing?

LIN: Neither of them works, you know.

KEN: How come?

LIN: One's lazy and just sponges off his parents, and the other has a screw loose and can't hold a job.

On Your Own

Work with a partner. Choose three idioms. Write a short conversation for each idiom. Then act out your conversations.

Discussion

Work with a partner or in a small group. Do the following activities.

1. What are the household items found in the idioms in this unit? Can you explain what these items are used for?

2. What idioms in your native language use household items and tools? Are any idioms like the ones in English?

3. If you **take potluck** as an unexpected guest, you eat whatever the others eat at the table. How do people in your native country treat an unexpected guest? How do they treat an expected guest?

4. People watch **soap operas** on television. Do you know any popular soap operas? Describe them.

Idioms from Medicine

Reading

Read the story. Then discuss the questions.

A Lot of Nerve

I like birds. They're beautiful when they fly. Many of them have lovely colors. But I was **sick and tired** of that pigeon. It caused too much trouble.

It really **had a lot of nerve.** Every morning it came to my backyard and ate all the baby lettuces one by one. It was very careful to eat the best. It **took great pains** to do so. And so I decided to stop its mischief. I wanted to give the bird **a taste of its own medicine.**

I built the ugliest-looking scarecrow you ever saw. I dressed it in old clothes and put it in the yard. Would it work? I really wasn't sure. I **felt it in my bones** that the bird might know it was a trick.

The next day I decided to see what was happening. I paused for a moment, **held my breath,** and looked out the window. There in the middle of the yard was the pigeon pulling out straws from the hat on my scarecrow. And I could see that more lettuce had been eaten. Clearly, I had to think of a new plan.

1. When you're **sick and tired** of something, how do you feel about the thing? What things are you sick and tired of doing?

2. If you **have a lot of nerve,** are you shy?

3. When you **take great pains** to do something, how do you do it? What do you take great pains about doing?

Meanings

Each example has an idiom from medicine. Read the example carefully to find the meaning of the idiom. Then look at the definitions that follow the examples. Write the idiom next to its definition.

blood is thicker than water

Anna gave her son the job instead of advertising the position. You know, **blood is thicker than water.**

a bitter pill to swallow

When Bob lost his job after working with the same company for ten years, it was **a bitter pill to swallow.**

to cough up

Cough up the rent or leave the apartment.

to feel it in one's bones

Our team's going to win the game. I can **feel it in my bones.**

a fly in the ointment

We want to buy a house, but there's just **one fly in the ointment.** We don't have enough money for a down payment.

to get burned

If you invest a lot of money in the stock market, you may **get burned** and lose your money.

to give someone a taste of his/her own medicine

If Lena keeps on shouting at people and getting angry, someone will **give her a taste of her own medicine** and shout back at her.

to have a lot of nerve

Elmer **has a lot of nerve.** He got a pay raise three months ago. Now he's asking for another one.

to hold one's breath

If you're angry, **hold your breath** and count to ten. After that, you'll feel calmer.

sick and tired

I am **sick and tired** of doing all the housework myself. I need some help.

to take pains

If you **take pains** to do something well, it will often be a success. And you won't have to take time to do it over, because it will be right the first time.

1. _____   very annoyed, very tired of doing something

2. _____ relatives are the most important people
_____

3. _____ to act so badly and impolitely that it actually takes courage to do so

4. _____ to take a lot of trouble to do something

5. _____ to do something bad to someone after the other person has done the same bad thing
_____

6. _____ to know something, often before seeing it or before it happens
_____

7. _____ to pause, to stop and think

8. _____ something difficult and unpleasant to experience
_____

9. _____ to pay money

10. _____ to have a bad experience, to be cheated

11. _____ a problem

Practice

A. Answer each question with **yes** or **no.** Explain your answer.

1. Jill always does things fast and makes mistakes. Does she take pains with her work?

2. My grandfather always knows when trouble is coming. Can he feel it in his bones?

3. Beth put sugar in my soup. If I put some in hers, will she get a taste of her own medicine?

4. Ernie watches television seven hours each day. Is he sick and tired of television?

5. After training hard, Sheree came in last in her race. Was this a bitter pill to swallow?

6. Carol never pays her bills. Does she cough up easily?

7. Carol didn't pay me back when I lent her money. Does that mean I got burned?

8. We were able to get tickets to the big game, but they were in the last row and we couldn't see very well. Was there a fly in the ointment somewhere?

9. That person walked right to the head of the line, before the rest of us who were waiting. Did he have a lot of nerve?

10. If you're making a lot of mistakes, is it a good idea to stop and hold your breath before continuing?

11. The doctor gave the job of receptionist to his niece. Does this show that blood is thicker than water?

B. Complete each example with an idiom from this unit.

1. I hurried to get to the game on time, but there was a

   _____. The game was

   on Tuesday, not Monday.

2. You _____ to take my

   English book without telling me.

3. Enrique always _____

   to make sure that he does his assignments on time.

4. It's going to rain. I

   _____.

5. I'm _____ of getting

   junk mail every day.

6. You know _____ when

   it comes to choosing someone for a job.

7. Basil always played tricks on Victoria. Then, one day, Victoria

   played a trick on Basil. He

   _____.

8. I didn't get the job because I was overqualified and had too

   much experience. It was a

   _____.

9. You've been trying to figure out the answers to these questions for the last two hours. Why not stop and

_____ and then try

again?

10. Never buy a car with lots of miles on it without a guarantee. Otherwise, you'll probably

_____ .

11. Whenever we collect money in class for a party or anything else, there are some students who don't

_____ .

Conversation

Practice each conversation with a partner.

SITUATION 1

Two friends are talking about Eve.

SUE-ELLEN: Did you hear about Eve's car?

JOLYNNE: You mean the one that stopped in the middle of the highway?

SUE-ELLEN: Yes. She really got burned when she bought it cheap.

SITUATION 2

The conversation continues. The friends are getting ready to go to school.

JOLYNNE: Sue-Ellen, stop rushing around. You're only wasting time.

SUE-ELLEN: But I can't remember what I need to take with me.

JOLYNNE: Calm down. Hold your breath, count to ten, and try to remember again.

SITUATION 3

The conversation continues. The friends are on their way to school.

SUE-ELLEN: I'm not going to do well on the test.

JOLYNNE: How do you know?

SUE-ELLEN: I don't. I just feel it in my bones.

On Your Own

Work with a partner. Choose three idioms. Write a short conversation for each idiom. Then act out your conversations.

Discussion

Work with a partner or in a small group. Do the following activities.

1. Look over the idioms in this unit. Which words relate to medicine? Can you tell the meanings of those words?

2. The idioms in this unit all use words from medicine. Do you know any other English idioms that use words from medicine?

3. Are there medicine idioms in your native language? Are any idioms like the ones in English?

4. Describe a situation where you or someone you know **got burned.**

UNIT 12

Idioms from Plants

Reading

Read the story. Then discuss the questions.

Undecided

Eustacia always wanted her life to be **a bed of roses.** She wanted everything to be easy and comfortable. But when she had a choice or decision to make, she could not do it. When you asked her what she was going to do, she always **beat around the bush.** She never gave a direct answer. And when she did decide something, she usually made a mistake. She was always **barking up the wrong tree.** So, she decided **to turn over a new leaf** and change her life. But when she finally made up her mind to change, she couldn't decide what to do. That was **the last straw.** She realized that she would never change. **In a nutshell,** if you want to describe Eustacia, you could say that she isn't good at making decisions.

1. What do you do when you **beat around the bush**?

2. When you decide to **turn over a new leaf,** what do you do? Have you ever turned over a new leaf? What did you decide to do?

3. If you describe something **in a nutshell,** do you give a long explanation or a short explanation?

Meanings

Each example has an idiom with a plant. Read the example carefully to find the meaning of the idiom. Then look at the definitions that follow the examples. Write the idiom next to its definition.

to bark up the wrong tree	If you think I'm responsible, you're **barking up the wrong tree.** You should be talking to my partner. She made the decision.
to beat around the bush	Please don't **beat around the bush.** Just answer my question yes or no.
a bed of roses	My job is no **bed of roses.** I get a good salary, but I have to work long hours.
bushed	I've been working nonstop for ten hours. I'm really **bushed.**
to hit the hay	I'm very tired and it's late. So I'm going **to hit the hay.**
in a nutshell	I don't have time to tell you the whole story now, but **in a nutshell,** Sally's getting married and moving to New York.
the last straw	Everything's gone badly this week, and today I lost my wallet! That's **the last straw.**
to nip something in the bud	I've been eating too much this week, and I'm gaining weight. I'd better **nip the habit in the bud** and start eating less.
through the grapevine	I heard **through the grapevine** that you're moving to New York. Is it true?
to turn over a new leaf	James decided **to turn over a new leaf.** This time he would not make the same mistakes.
up a tree	I'm **up a tree** with this homework assignment. I just don't know how to do it.

1. _____   a comfortable, easy situation

2. _____   to waste time by not giving
   _____   a direct answer

3. _____   to make the wrong choice and waste
   _____   one's efforts

4. _____   to start over again, to start a new and better life

5. _____   the final thing after a series of bad things, the thing that finally makes you angry

6. _____   in a few words

7. _____   to stop something when it's just beginning

8. _____   from what one person said to another, by rumor

9. _____   in a difficult situation from which you cannot find a way out

10. _____   to go to bed and sleep

11. _____   very tired, exhausted

Practice

A. Answer each question with **yes** or **no.** Explain your answer.

1. Our boss spent the whole afternoon telling us why we couldn't have a raise in salary this year. Did he say it in a nutshell?

2. Luis used to study only before tests. Then he failed a course. Now he studies three hours every day. Did he turn over a new leaf?

3. Berta has to work ten hours a day, six days a week in a factory for very little pay. Is her life a bed of roses?

4. Kenji didn't go to work today. He went to the beach and relaxed. Is he bushed tonight?

5. On the six o'clock news, it was announced that the football coach was going to retire. Did we hear this news through the grapevine?

6. Leo went into the yard to do some work. Did he hit the hay?

7. Things have been going well in Howard's life, but today he lost his keys. Was this the last straw?

8. Little Laura liked to jump up and down on the sofa. Her Momma soon stopped that. Did Momma nip the habit in the bud?

9. Brent loves to watch the trees move in the wind. Is he up a tree?

10. Jenny wanted a new bicycle. So she asked her older sister if she had any money. Her older sister never has any money. Was Jenny barking up the wrong tree?

11. When we asked our boss whether we were going to get raises, she talked about the problems the company was having and didn't give us a clear answer. Did the boss beat around the bush?

B. Each example has the correct idiom, but there is one error with each idiom. Find the error and correct it.

1. We had no time to lose, so they told us in nutshell.

2. If you think she'll help us, you're barking at the wrong tree.

3. Andrew forgot his keys for the third day in a row. It was last straw for Andrew.

4. Ken had a terrible problem. He was in a tree.

5. Elizabeth's family was very rich. She didn't have to work. Life was a bed of rose for her.

6. After working for twelve hours today to finish the job, Todd was bush.

7. Let's not beat in the bush. Let's decide right now.

8. After Bud got a new job, he turned into a new leaf.

9. We have to nip this problem in the buds by making a statement to the public.

10. Joan was very tired, so she hit a hay at eight o'clock last night.

11. We heard on the vine that we're getting new computers in our office.

Conversation

Practice each conversation with a partner.

SITUATION 1

Frank and Antonio are trying to raise money to help a sick student.

FRANK: Is Paul going to help us?

ANTONIO: He told me all about the problems he's having. In a nutshell, he says he can't help us.

SITUATION 2

Two friends are talking after school.

BOB: Do you want to go out with us tonight?

JO: Sorry. I'm going to hit the hay early tonight. I'm really bushed.

SITUATION 3

Maria is with Amy, who is angry and upset.

AMY: What a week! First, I lost my wallet, then my car broke down, and now I broke my glasses.

MARIA: Oh no, the lights just went out!

AMY: That's the last straw! I'm going to go to bed and forget my problems.

On Your Own

Work with a partner. Choose three idioms. Write a short conversation for each idiom. Then act out your conversations.

Discussion

Work with a partner or in a small group. Do the following activities.

1. What idioms in your native language use plant words? Are any idioms like the ones in English?

2. **To be bushed** means to be exhausted. Were you bushed recently? Tell why.

3. Did you ever **bark up the wrong tree** when you wanted something? Describe what happened.

UNIT 13

Idioms from Clothes

Reading

Read the story. Then discuss the questions.

In the Boss's Shoes

Some people get angry easily. You have to be careful and **handle them with kid gloves.** My boss is always angry. He's always **hot under the collar** about something. If sales are bad, he gets very nervous. He's afraid that he's going to lose everything. He thinks he's about **to lose his shirt.** But the business never makes very much money. We always run **on a shoestring.** In business, you have to be calm and keep your temper. You have **to keep your shirt on.** Our business might be better if my boss could stay calm. Still, I prefer to be me than to have my boss's job. I don't want **to be in his shoes.** He's under too much pressure.

1. If you get **hot under the collar,** how do you feel? What makes you get hot under the collar?

2. If you **keep your shirt on,** do you get hot under the collar?

3. Many people would like **to be in someone else's shoes.** Whose shoes would you like to be in?

Meanings

Each example has an idiom with clothes. Read the example carefully to find the meaning of the idiom. Then look at the definitions that follow the examples. Write the idiom next to its definition.

to be in someone else's shoes

I wouldn't like **to be in Leroy's shoes** when Dad comes home and sees that broken window.

dressed to kill

Blodwyn went to the party **dressed to kill** in his new black suit, silk shirt, and red tie.

a feather in one's cap

Passing the driver's test on the first try was a real **feather in my cap.**

to handle someone with kid gloves

The president has a difficult personality, and she gets angry easily. You have **to handle her with kid gloves.**

hot under the collar

Mike had an important meeting in another city. He got **hot under the collar** because the plane was late taking off.

to keep one's shirt on

I'll finish using the computer in a minute. Just **keep your shirt on,** and you'll get your turn.

to keep something under one's hat

I'm getting married, but **keep it under your hat.** I don't want anyone to know yet.

to lose one's shirt

Bob invested a lot of money in stocks and **lost his shirt.**

on a shoestring

Alice started a business although she didn't have very much money. She's running it **on a shoestring.**

a stuffed shirt

Higgins is such **a stuffed shirt.** He always wears a tie, and he even eats chicken with a knife and fork.

tied to someone's apron strings

Basil never does anything unless his mother says it's okay. He's **tied to her apron strings.**

1. _____ angry

2. _____ with very little money

3. _____ not to get angry, to be patient

4. _____ to be careful not to anger someone
   _____

5. _____ to lose a lot of money

6. _____ to be in the place of someone else
   _____

7. _____ in one's best clothes and looking good

8. _____   always following a stronger person

   _____

9. _____   someone who lives by the rules and is
                                         very formal

10. _____   something to be proud of and to feel
                                          good about

11. _____   to keep something secret

    _____

Practice

A. Answer each question with **yes** or **no**. Explain your answer.

1. Is getting a speeding ticket a feather in your cap?

2. Is it a waste of energy getting hot under the collar?

3. If you handle someone with kid gloves, do you treat the person well?

4. If you do something on a shoestring, do you spend a lot of money?

5. If you want a more interesting job like one a friend of yours has, do you want to be in someone else's shoes?

6. Would you call a rock singer a stuffed shirt?

7. Is a strong person tied to someone else's apron strings?

8. If you go on a picnic, do you dress to kill?

9. If you tell someone to keep his or her shirt on, are you telling the person to hurry up?

10. You told everyone the news. Did you keep it under your hat?

11. If you lose your shirt, are you an untidy person?

B. Complete each example with an idiom from this unit.

1. Clarence is no fun. He's just a

   _____ .

2. Winning the contest is a real

   _____ for you.

3. Dave _____ gambling

   on the stock market.

4. I sometimes wish I were

_____.

5. It's no use getting

_____ for nothing.

6. Tex is such a wimp. He's still

_____ to his mother's

_____.

7. When I was a student, I always lived

_____.

8. You can tell Jane my secret. You know that she'll

_____.

9. _____. I'll be ready in

a minute.

10. Gloria looks great tonight. She's

_____.

11. Mom is angry about something. We'd better

_____.

Conversation

Practice each conversation with a partner.

SITUATION 1

Two workers are talking.

    ANDY: Are you afraid of Mr. Parker?

    RINGO: No. Why?

    ANDY: You always seem to treat him with kid gloves. That's why.

SITUATION 2

The conversation continues.

RINGO: Well, Parker is a stuffed shirt.

ANDY: Yes, but that's no reason to look as if you're tied to his apron strings.

SITUATION 3

The conversation continues.

RINGO: Would you like to be in my shoes? I have to do everything he asks and more.

ANDY: Keep your shirt on. I didn't ask you to take the job.

RINGO: Okay. Let's talk about something else.

On Your Own

Work with a partner. Choose three idioms. Write a short conversation for each idiom. Then act out your conversations.

Discussion

Work with a partner or in a small group. Do the following activities.

1. The idioms in this unit all use clothes. Do you know any other English idioms that use clothes?

2. Are there clothes idioms in your native language? Are any idioms like the ones in English?

3. Would you like to be in the shoes of a stuffed shirt who was tied to his or her mother's apron strings? Say why not.

4. Describe a situation where you wouldn't like to be in someone else's shoes.

UNIT 14

Idioms from Time

Reading

Read the story. Then discuss the questions.

Cat Time

My cat is an expert at waiting for things to happen. Waiting around and **killing time** is her specialty. She watches the birds in the backyard for a couple of hours at a time.

Like all cats, she never makes plans. She'll do many things **on the spur of the moment.** For example, if she suddenly feels that **the time is right,** she'll try to go fishing in my fish tank.

Her favorite hobby is tree climbing. Give her a dangerous tree and she won't hesitate. **In no time,** I'll have to call the fire department to come and get her down. When she hears the fire engine, she gets scared and jumps out of the tree. She always lands on her four feet **in the nick of time**—just before she hits the ground. Then she walks away as if there's no problem.

1. When you **kill time,** what are you doing? What do you do when you want to kill time?

2. When you do something **on the spur of the moment,** do you plan it in advance? When is the last time you went somewhere on the spur of the moment?

3. If you do something **in the nick of time,** do you do it before it's too late or after it's too late?

Meanings

Each example has an idiom with time. Read the example carefully to find the meaning of the idiom. Then look at the definitions that follow the examples. Write the idiom next to its definition.

the big time Mafalda used to work in a supermarket. Then she hit **the big time** and she got a job as the star actress in a movie.

to call it a day When I finish writing this composition, I'm going **to call it a day** and go to bed.

for the time being We have no extra money. So **for the time being,** we can't move to a nicer apartment.

high time It's **high time** we bought a new car. The old one keeps dying out on the highway.

in no time When Sid got sick suddenly, we called the emergency number and the paramedics were here **in no time.**

in the nick of time The vase was just about to fall off the sink, but she grabbed it **in the nick of time,** so it didn't break.

to kill time We were a half hour early for the movie. To **kill time,** we went to the fast-food restaurant next door for a cup of coffee.

to make time I was planning to work on my report all day, but I'll **make time** in the morning to meet with you and discuss the problem.

on the spur of the moment They didn't plan to go away for the weekend. They decided to go to the mountains **on the spur of the moment.**

to take one's time It's better **to take your time** when doing tests than to hurry and make mistakes.

the time is right **The time is right** to invest in a house because real estate prices are low now.

1. _____ to waste time, waiting for something else to happen

2. _____ quickly

3. _____ immediately, without planning

4. _____ it is a good time to do something

5. _____ just before it is too late

6. _____ not to hurry

7. _____ to do something although you did not plan it and you are already busy

8. _____ almost too late to do something

9. _____ a high level of success

10. _____ to stop doing something

11. _____ temporarily, just for the present moment

Practice

A. Answer each question with **yes** or **no**. Explain your answer.

1. Fernando had half a tank of gasoline, but he still went to the gas station to fill his tank up. Did he go just in the nick of time?

2. Claudia was very busy when I gave her my letter to type. She said it wasn't a problem and typed it immediately. Did Claudia make time to type my letter?

3. It was six o'clock in the evening. We were very tired, but we were determined to finish the project, even if it meant staying up all night. Did we call it a day at six?

4. Joanna wrote a romance novel, and she suddenly became famous and very rich. Did she hit the big time?

5. We had nothing to do on the long train trip, so we played cards. Did we play cards to kill time?

6. When we called room service at the hotel to get some coffee, it came two hours later. Did it come in no time?

7. There's no safe place to sit on Tony's sofa. It's falling to pieces. Is it high time he got a new one?

8. We always plan our vacation at least six months ahead of time. Do we go on vacation on the spur of the moment?

9. Car prices are at their lowest. Is the time right to buy a new car?

10. We were already twenty minutes late, but Jackie still didn't rush to get ready. Did she take her time?

11. Irina was thinking about moving to the suburbs, but she's decided to stay in the city for a while. Is she staying in the city for the time being?

B. Each example has the correct idiom, but there is one error with each idiom. Find the error and correct it.

1. It's higher time he got himself a job.

2. I think we've done a lot of work. Let's call a day.

3. We're staying at my sister's house for the time be.

4. The police came at no time.

5. We watched TV to kill the time, while we waited for the cab.

6. That singer is in big time now.

7. Robin made time to check over my composition.

8. We went to the movies on the spur of moment.

9. He came with the money in nick of time.

10. The times is right to buy a house.

11. I like to take my times in the morning and not hurry off to work.

Conversation

Practice each conversation with a partner.

SITUATION 1

Ntozake is talking to her secretary at the office.

NTOZAKE: Ginny, I wonder if you could type this memo for me.

GINNY: I can do it in no time.

NTOZAKE: No need to hurry. Take your time.

SITUATION 2

Pat and Joyce are going to see a movie.

PAT: We're almost one hour early. What should we do to kill time?

JOYCE: Well, there's a coffee shop across the street.

PAT: Great! We can take our time over a cup of coffee.

SITUATION 3

Tim and Ben are working together on a project at the office.

TIM: I'm really tired.

BEN: Me too. Let's leave the project as it is for the time being.

TIM: I'm glad you want to call it a day too.

On Your Own

Work with a partner. Choose three idioms. Write a short conversation for each idiom. Then act out your conversations.

Discussion

Work with a partner or in a small group. Do the following activities.

1. The idioms in this unit use words with time. Do you know any other idioms in English that use words with time?

2. When you have time and nothing special to do, you **kill time.** How do people kill time in your native country?

3. **In the nick of time** means just before it's too late. Tell a story using this idiom.

UNIT 15

Idioms from the Weather

Reading

Read the story. Then discuss the questions.

A Breeze

For some folks, everything is easy. Life is a **breeze.** They're always healthy. They're never **under the weather.** If they walk into a room full of strangers, they make friends in five minutes. They have no trouble **breaking the ice.** They earn enough to save some money every week. They're **saving money for a rainy day.** So if trouble ever does come, they'll be able **to weather the storm.** Yes, some people have no problems if times are good or bad. They're okay **come rain or shine.**

1. If something is **a breeze,** is it easy or hard for you to do? What things are a breeze for you?

2. If you're **under the weather,** how do you feel?

3. When you **break the ice,** what do you do?

Meanings

Each example has an idiom from the weather. Read the example carefully to find the meaning of the idiom. Then look at the definitions that follow the examples. Write the idiom next to its definition.

to break the ice   Cedric is very shy. If he goes to a party where he doesn't know anyone, he finds it very hard **to break the ice.**

a breeze   Because I studied English every day, the exam was **a breeze.**

come rain or shine   Uncle Jeremiah lives two hundred miles away, but he'll be at my birthday party **come rain or shine.**

a fair-weather friend   Judy showed that she was just **a fair-weather friend.** When I needed help on my report, she refused.

full of hot air   Many politicians are **full of hot air.** They make promises, but they don't keep them.

to have one's head in the clouds   I don't think Celia understands that she's in danger of not passing the course. She seems **to have her head in the clouds.**

to rain cats and dogs   It must be **raining cats and dogs** outside. The rain's pounding on the roof.

to save something for a rainy day   Hank makes only four hundred dollars a week, but every week he **saves forty for a rainy day.**

snowed under   I have to stay late at the office tonight and finish some things because I'm **snowed under** with work.

under the weather   Berta was feeling **under the weather,** so she didn't go to work.

to weather the storm   Our business has had a lot of problems this year. But I'm sure things will be okay if we can **weather the storm** for just a few more months.

1. _____   something easy for a person to do

2. _____   sick

3. _____   to begin a conversation with a stranger

4. _____   no matter how hard it is to do

5. _____   to prepare for trouble, usually by saving money

6. _____   to wait and be patient until things get better

7. _____   talking a lot but never doing what one says

8. _____   not to know or understand what is
   _____   going on

9. _____   to rain very hard

10. _____   having a lot of work to do

11. _____   a person who doesn't help when a friend
    is in trouble

Practice

A. Answer each question with **yes** or **no**. Explain your answer.

1. In the first year, the business didn't do well, but the second year it did better. Did the business weather the storm?

2. The rain was very light, so Tim went jogging as usual. Was it raining cats and dogs when Tim went jogging?

3. A teenager and an older woman were sitting opposite each other in a train compartment. After about two hours, the teenager asked the woman if she was going to New Jersey, and the woman answered. Did the teenager break the ice?

4. Julia has two big assignments due next Monday, and she's just starting on them. Is she snowed under?

5. The politician promised no taxes and free health care for everybody. But when she was elected, she didn't keep the promises. Was she full of hot air?

6. Rob doesn't have any money saved. He spends everything. Does he save something for a rainy day?

7. Louisa lent me some money when I needed it to pay my tuition bill. Was she a fair-weather friend?

8. Penny thought she was getting a cold and didn't go out with her friends last night. Was she feeling under the weather?

9. Geraldo is gifted at learning languages. After six months in the United States, he spoke perfect English. Was learning English a breeze for Geraldo?

10. You can always depend on Ngogi to do what he says. He keeps his promises even if it's hard for him. Does Ngogi keep his promises come rain or shine?

11. Some of my classmates don't think about or plan for the future. They seem to think everything will work out with no effort on their part. Do they have their heads in the clouds?

B. Complete the idiom in each example with the correct word or words.

1. Alexei wasn't shy and broke _____ ice at the party.

2. You can't go out. It's raining _____ and _____.

3. I should have finished this composition last week because now I'm snowed _____.

4. Sid doesn't seem to pay attention in class. He has his head _____ _____ clouds.

5. I'll finish this come rain _____ shine.

6. Katrina's feeling _____ _____ weather today.

7. You should save some for _____ rainy _____.

8. The entrance exam was _____ breeze.

9. We have no other choice but to weather _____ _____.

10. Craig is full _____ hot _____.

11. Rosa helped me when I needed it. She was not a _____-weather friend.

Conversation

Practice each conversation with a partner.

SITUATION 1

Will is calling Angie in New York.

WILL: How's the weather in New York?

ANGIE: It's raining cats and dogs right now.

WILL: Do you think the weather will be better tomorrow when I get there?

ANGIE: The weather report says we'll be in for a cold spell starting tomorrow.

SITUATION 2

Bonnie calls her classmate Nancy.

BONNIE: I didn't see you in class today. Are you okay?

NANCY: I'm feeling a little under the weather.

BONNIE: I hope it's not serious.

NANCY: I think it's just the flu.

BONNIE: Well, take care and I hope you'll feel better soon.

SITUATION 3

Harry is asking Bob to play tennis.

HARRY: Are you coming to play tennis with us, Bob?

BOB: Sorry, I'm snowed under. I have to finish this work for tomorrow come rain or shine.

HARRY: Okay, Bob. I'll call you later.

On Your Own

Work with a partner. Choose three idioms. Write a short conversation for each idiom. Then act out your conversations.

Discussion

Work with a partner or in a small group. Do the following activities.

1. Are there any idioms in your native language that use words related to weather? Are any idioms like the ones in English?

2. **Raining cats and dogs** is an idiom that describes the weather. What idioms do you use to describe the weather in your native language?

3. **To weather the storm** means to wait and be patient until things get better. Describe a situation where you had to weather the storm.

4. When you do something no matter how hard it is, you do it **come rain or shine.** When did you do something come rain or shine?

Idioms from around the House

Reading

Read the story. Then discuss the questions.

Bringing Down the House

At the age of twenty-two, Ron decided that he wanted to become a comedian. When he told his father, the old man **hit the ceiling.** Ron's father shouted that Ron was throwing his college education **down the drain** and that he would end up as a bum. But Ron was serious about his career. He **took steps** to become a good comic. He studied acting, talked to comedians, and kept a book of jokes. He soon **got his foot in the door** and was performing in comedy clubs. And soon his act was **bringing down the house.** The audience would laugh and clap at all of Ron's jokes.

Ron ended up in the big time, as a major celebrity. This fact **hit home** when he returned to our town earlier this year. The town rolled out the red carpet for him. There was a big parade, and everything in town was **on the house** for Ron. Now, even Ron's father laughs at his jokes.

1. When someone **hits the ceiling,** how does the person feel?

2. What does it mean **to get your foot in the door**?

3. When a performer **brings down the house,** how does the audience react?

Meanings

Each example has an idiom with a word from around the house. Read the example carefully to find the meaning of the idiom. Then look at the definitions below. Write the idiom next to its definition.

to bring down the house

The comedian's jokes **brought down the house.** The audience wouldn't stop laughing.

down the drain

You've already spent a lot of money fixing your old car. Spending more is just money **down the drain.**

to drive someone up the wall

If you play loud music late at night, you'll **drive your neighbors up the wall.**

to get one's foot in the door

You should take any job in that company, just **to get your foot in the door.** Then you can work your way up to a better job.

to hit home

The problems of the economy really **hit home** when I lost my job.

to hit the ceiling

Humphrey **hit the ceiling** when he realized his car had been stolen again.

on the fence

I'm **on the fence** about whether I should continue school or get a full-time job.

on the house

At our local restaurant, customers get dessert **on the house** if they order a meal.

on the shelf

Some people feel **on the shelf** after they retire and no longer work. They don't feel needed anymore.

to take steps

We have to **take steps** to repair the roof before it rains again.

under the table

It's against the law to take money **under the table** to vote for someone.

1. _____ free, for nothing

2. _____ to make someone really realize something

3. _____ to suddenly become very angry

4. _____ wasted, lost

5. _____ to make someone angry or crazy

_____

6. _____ undecided

7. _____ to do something

8. _____ secretly, usually doing something against the law

9. _____ too old, no longer of use

10. _____
    _____ to take the first steps to start something, to get an opening

11. _____
    _____ to make an audience clap and laugh enthusiastically

Practice

A. Answer each question with **yes** or **no**. Explain your answer.

1. After the meal at the restaurant, we got free chocolates. Were the chocolates on the house?

2. Even though the election is tomorrow, many voters still haven't decided on the candidate they're going to vote for. Are many voters still on the fence?

3. The stand-up comic went onstage and told his jokes. The audience thought he was not that funny. Did he bring down the house?

4. In many professions, it is hard to get a first job and gain some experience in the field. Is it hard to get one's foot in the door?

5. When Sami told his father about his car accident, his father was very understanding and lent him some money for the repairs. Did his father hit the ceiling?

6. The neighbors' television is on so loud that I can't work. Is the neighbors' television driving me up the wall?

7. The construction company gave the mayor money so that it would be chosen to build the new highway. Did the mayor get money under the table?

8. During the exam the teacher made us sit in every other seat, we had nothing on our desks except the examination paper, and the teacher walked up and down the rows of seats during the exam. Did the teacher take steps to stop cheating?

9. Lane fell asleep during the president's speech. Did the president's speech hit home?

10. After he retired at age sixty-five, Harold didn't have anything to do and was very bored. Did he feel on the shelf?

11. Karl worked several weeks on the project, but then the project was canceled. Was Karl's work down the drain?

B. Each example has the correct idiom, but there is one error with each idiom. Find the error and correct it.

1. The coffee was in the house.

2. Her words about the importance of education hit the home.

3. All that money went down in the drain.

4. That dripping faucet is driving up the wall me.

5. Kate got her feet in the door as a secretary, and now she is a manager in the company.

6. Aunt Margie thinks she's been left on the shelves.

7. The pop singer was so good, she brought the house.

8. When my boss heard the news, he hit ceiling.

9. The school took step to prevent a fire hazard.

10. The mayor received some money under the table.

11. Sofia was above the fence. She couldn't decide whether to take the job.

Conversation

Practice each conversation with a partner.

SITUATION 1

Ted's in a small newly opened restaurant.

WAITER: Is everything fine, sir?

TED: Wonderful, thank you.

WAITER: And this is our special dessert. It's on the house.

SITUATION 2

Sal is talking to his wife, Jodie.

SAL: You look very tired.

JODIE: I am. I couldn't sleep all night. The neighbors' dog was barking. It drove me up the wall.

SAL: I didn't hear anything.

SITUATION 3

BART: I just dropped my father's camera and it broke.

JIM: Oh, no. What are you going to tell your father?

BART: Nothing. He'll hit the ceiling if he finds out.

On Your Own

Work with a partner. Choose three idioms. Write a short conversation for each idiom. Then act out your conversations.

Discussion

Work with a partner or in a small group. Do the following activities.

1. What idioms in your native language use house words? Are any idioms like the ones in English?

2. **To drive someone up the wall** means to make someone angry or crazy. What things drive you up the wall?

3. **To hit the ceiling** means to suddenly become very angry. Tell a story using this idiom.

Idioms with the Word *As*

Reading

Read the story. Then discuss the questions.

As Fit as a Fiddle

I had the flu last week. I was **as sick as a dog.** After four days in bed, I was **as weak as a kitten.** I barely had the strength to get out of bed. My friend Clarence called me every morning and evening to see if I needed anything. His calls were **as regular as clockwork.** At first, my fever would not go away. It was **as stubborn as a mule.** Then I began to feel better. On day five I was **as hungry as a bear.** All I wanted was food. Now I'm fine. I'm **as fit as a fiddle.**

1. When you're **as sick as a dog,** how sick are you?

2. When you're **as stubborn as a mule,** how stubborn are you?

3. When you're **as hungry as a bear,** how hungry are you?

4. What grammar form do you see in all the idioms in the reading? What meaning do you think the **as . . . as** gives to the adjective (**sick, stubborn, hungry**) in the phrase?

Meanings

Each example has an idiom with a comparison using **as.** Read the example carefully to find the meaning of the idiom. Then look at the definitions below. Write the idiom next to its definition.

as busy as a bee   Maxine is always working, either at home or at the office. She's **as busy as a bee.**

as fit as a fiddle   Bart trains two hours every day. At sixty-eight, he's **as fit as a fiddle.**

as good as gold   Baby-sitting for my little nephew Elrod was no trouble at all. In fact, he was **as good as gold.**

as happy as a lark   When Marcus got engaged to be married, he was **as happy as a lark.**

as hard as nails   The teacher is **as hard as nails.** He's strict and accepts no excuses from students who do not do their work.

as hungry as a bear   Every time I exercise, I'm **as hungry as a bear** afterward, and I eat a big snack.

as plain as day   Every week they spend more than they earn. It's **as plain as day** that they need to spend less and go on a budget.

as regular as clockwork   Dylan catches the same bus at the same time every day. He's **as regular as clockwork.**

as sick as a dog   After I ate that bad shrimp, I was **as sick as a dog.**

as stubborn as a mule   Maisie is **as stubborn as a mule.** She doesn't like broccoli and she won't eat it even if you pay her.

as weak as a kitten   After she was ill in bed for three weeks, Penny was **as weak as a kitten.**

1. _____   not willing to change one's mind, very set in one's ideas

2. _____   very healthy

3. _____   very hungry

4. _____   not very strong

5. _____   very unwell

6. _____   always at the same time

7. _____   very good, well-behaved

8. _____   very busy

9. _____   very easy to see or understand

10. _____ very hard and cold, not forgiving

11. _____ very happy

Practice

A. Answer each question with **yes** or **no.** Explain your answer.

1. Tina's new baby doesn't cry. She sleeps and smiles most of the time. Is the baby as good as gold?

2. Doug has been in bed for a week now with a very bad flu. Is he as sick as a dog?

3. Dennis tries hard, but he's never on time. You never know when he's going to appear. Is he as regular as clockwork?

4. Nina didn't pass her final exam. Do you think she's as happy as a lark?

5. Louise runs five miles every day, and she watches what she eats. Is she as fit as a fiddle?

6. Gina is always running around doing something, either at home or in the office. Is she as busy as a bee?

7. Kim's father never forgave her for taking his car and then getting a speeding ticket. He said he'll never let her use the car again, and he means it. Is Kim's father as hard as nails?

8. After walking in the fresh country air, Melinda came back and had a small salad for lunch. Was she as hungry as a bear?

9. We asked Ahmed if he wanted to go to the movies with us yesterday. He didn't really want to, but we persuaded him to come. Was Ahmed as stubborn as a mule?

10. Max, who weighs 250 pounds and lifts weights, had surgery a few days ago. When we went to see him, he didn't have the energy to get up. Was he as weak as a kitten?

11. Ed has stayed up every night for a week to do his report. Now he looks very tired and has dark circles under his eyes. Is it as plain as day that Ed needs a rest?

B. Each example has the correct idiom, but there is one error with each idiom. Find the error and correct it.

1. My sister Katie is as stubborn as mule. You can never change her mind.

2. I started to jog and exercise every day, and now I'm as fit as the fiddle.

3. It's as plain as a day he needs to wear glasses.

4. My brother always comes home as hungry like a bear.

5. My mother is always as busy as bees in the house.

6. I get to work at eight every morning as regular as clockworks.

7. The baby-sitter said little Timmy was as good like gold.

8. Don was as sick as dog yesterday.

9. It's good to see her as happy as a lake.

10. Berta is as hard nails. She's very strict.

11. After the operation, I felt as weak as the kitten.

Conversation

Practice each conversation with a partner.

SITUATION 1

Two friends are talking.

LIN: Is Suzy coming with us?

PAM: I asked her three times already and she said no.

LIN: Forget it then. She's as stubborn as a mule. We'll go without her.

SITUATION 2

Two classmates are talking.

TRAN: Where were you last week?

BOB: Oh, I was as sick as a dog with the flu.

TRAN: Are you better now?

BOB: Sure am. As fit as a fiddle!

SITUATION 3

Ernie comes home after football practice.

ERNIE: What's for dinner, Mom?

MOM: There's roast chicken and ice cream for dessert.

ERNIE: I'm as hungry as a bear. Can I eat now?

On Your Own

Work with a partner. Choose three idioms. Write a short conversation for each idiom. Then act out your conversations.

Discussion

Work with a partner or in a small group. Do the following activities.

1. Do you know any other idioms in English with the word **as**? Make a list.

2. Are there idioms in your native language that use words like **as** to make comparisons? Are any idioms similar to the ones in English?

3. **As sick as a dog, as busy as a bee, as happy as a lark, as hungry as a bear, as weak as a kitten, as stubborn as a mule** are idioms that compare people to animals by using the word **as**. How true are these idioms? Is a lark (a kind of bird) happy? Are mules stubborn?

Idioms with Repetition

Reading

Read the story. Then discuss the questions.

A Fuddy-Duddy or a Hotshot?

A lot of people thought Uncle Max was crazy. He was always losing things in his **topsy-turvy** office where papers were scattered all over, or he was trying to explain some new scientific **mumbo jumbo** that no one else could understand. He was so **wishy-washy** that I once saw him waste ten minutes trying to decide whether to wear a blue shirt or a white one.

It was only later we discovered that the old **fuddy-duddy,** who spent most of his time alone with his books, was a very important scientist. He worked in a secret government operation. He was a **hotshot** rocket technician in one of the most **hush-hush** projects of this century.

1. If something is **topsy-turvy,** is it neat? Do you know of any places that are topsy-turvy?

2. If someone talks **mumbo jumbo,** is it clear to you?

3. If something is **hush-hush,** does everyone know about it?

Meanings

Each example has an idiom with repetition. Read the example carefully to find the meaning of the idiom. Then look at the definitions below. Write the idiom next to its definition.

to dillydally   If Debbie plans to come with us, we'd better get to her house an hour early. She always **dillydallies** when she's getting ready.

fuddy-duddy   Harold never goes anywhere new, always wears a tie, eats the same food every day, and is in bed by nine o'clock. He's a real **fuddy-duddy.**

hotshot   Jane thinks that she's a real **hotshot** driver, but she keeps getting tickets.

humdrum   We got tired of our **humdrum** routine and decided to take a week's vacation on a tropical island.

hush-hush   She works for the government, but nobody knows exactly what she does. Her job is very **hush-hush.**

mumbo jumbo   Have you tried to read and understand all that **mumbo jumbo** in the insurance policy?

pitter-patter   My neighbors Mamie and Jules are expecting a baby. So we'll soon be hearing the **pitter-patter** of tiny feet around the house.

tip-top   My aunt has always taken good care of her car. After eight years and only twenty-five thousand miles, it's in **tip-top** condition.

topsy-turvy   I can never find anything in this room. Everything is so **topsy-turvy.**

wishy-washy   My boss is very **wishy-washy.** He has trouble deciding who should do what, and he doesn't give clear orders.

a wheeler-dealer   Marvin is a big-time **wheeler-dealer** in real estate. He keeps buying and selling stores and hotels all over the country.

1. _____   secret

2. _____   someone who is very good at something, but who often isn't very modest

3. _____   undecided, weak, not definite and clear

4. _____   to hesitate, to waste time by moving slowly

5. _____   routine, repeated activities

6. _____   not organized, messy

7. _____   best

8. _____ a person who is always making business deals and trying to get the best deal

9. _____ language that cannot easily be understood, jargon

10. _____ sound of quick, light taps, like the sound of rain or children's feet

11. _____ someone who doesn't like change

Practice

A. Answer each question with **yes** or **no.** Explain your answer.

1. Bud plays the stock market, surfs, races horses, and eats out a lot. Is he a fuddy-duddy?

2. Sue always knows exactly what she wants and where she's going. Is she wishy-washy?

3. If you do the same thing at the same time in the same place every day, is your life humdrum?

4. If Ted doesn't like to bargain and always pays the full price for everything, is he a wheeler-dealer?

5. Yehudi scores the most points in every basketball game he plays and tells everybody after the game. Is he a hotshot?

6. My father is a mail carrier. Does he have a hush-hush job?

7. Bogblot wonglat floom grunk. Could that be mumbo jumbo?

8. Ed is always on time—always. Does he usually dillydally?

9. Everything in her room is neat and organized. Is it topsy-turvy?

10. The sounds of thunder rumbled through the sky. Was that a pitter-patter?

11. Sandy always does excellent work. Is her work tip-top?

B. Complete each example with an idiom from this unit.

1. I don't know exactly what kind of research my brother does. It's very _____.

2. I don't know how to work the videocassette recorder. I can't understand all that confusing

_____.

3. Be careful if you golf with Randy. He's quite a

    _____ at golf and he'll

    probably win.

4. The wind was so strong that everything in the yard ended up

    _____.

5. If you're going to win the race, you must be in

    _____ condition.

6. If you're quiet when it rains, you can hear the

    _____ of the raindrops

    on the windows or the roof.

7. I never know what my boss wants me to do first. He's so

    _____.

8. Are you going to _____

    all day here, or can we leave soon?

9. Marilyn's a real _____.

    She's always buying and selling something.

10. If Derek wants to be an old

    _____, let's go to the

    beach without him.

11. I do the same things every day. My life is so

    _____.

Conversation

Practice each conversation with a partner.

SITUATION 1

Two students are attending college classes.

    Tom: What did you think of the science lecture?

    Bob: To tell you the truth, it was mumbo jumbo to me.

    Tom: Well, I'm glad to know you think that, too.

SITUATION 2

The students are about to leave for class.

TOM: Don't dillydally or we'll be late for class!

BOB: I'm coming! Don't worry; we still have five minutes.

SITUATION 3

The students are talking about a party.

BOB: Guess who didn't come to the class party?

TOM: Edward.

BOB: Yes. He's such a fuddy-duddy.

On Your Own

Work with a partner. Choose three idioms. Write a short conversation for each idiom. Then act out your conversations.

Discussion

Work with a partner or in a small group. Do the following activities.

1. The idioms in this unit all use repetition. Do you know any other English idioms that use repetition?

2. Are there repetitive idioms in your native language? Are any idioms like the ones in English?

3. Why would you not trust a wheeler-dealer who spoke to you with a lot of technical mumbo jumbo?

UNIT 19

Idioms with Words That Go Together I

Reading

Read the story. Then discuss the questions.

A Big Puzzle

A while ago, I decided to put together one of those five thousand-piece jigsaw puzzles all by myself. I was sure that I could do it because I'm good at all kinds of games—from crossword puzzles to video games. But it wasn't so easy **after all.** First, I put all the pieces on the table, and I started to work on the sky part of the puzzle. But **every other** piece was blue and seemed to fit in the sky. I must have stared at the pieces for two hours. "**Take it easy,**" I told myself. "**Sooner or later** you'll put some pieces together." And I was right. **Before long,** I had several pieces together. But finishing the entire puzzle was a project that took me **quite a few** months. Of course, at the end, I learned the most important fact about putting together puzzles. The last piece is always missing! Just **the other day** I found that missing piece behind the sofa. **No wonder** I hadn't found it before!

1. When you tell someone to **take it easy,** how are you telling the person to act?

2. If something is going to happen **sooner or later,** will it happen immediately?

3. Does **quite a few** mean "many" or "not many"?

Meanings

Each example has an idiom made up of words that go together. Read the example carefully to find the meaning of the idiom. Then look at the definitions below. Write the idiom next to its definition. **Note:** You will use the same definition for two idioms.

above all
My mother told me to pack warm clothes for the trip, but **above all,** not to forget my toothbrush.

after all
I thought that I could complete my homework and go to the movie. But I didn't have time to do both **after all,** and I missed the movie.

before long
Isn't Doug here at the party yet? Don't worry. He's coming. He'll be here **before long.**

every other
One card for you. One card for me. One card for you. One card for me. . . . We each get **every other** one.

more or less
I've **more or less** finished painting the kitchen. There's just one small corner left.

never mind
Never mind about the broken vase. It wasn't very expensive, and I can buy another.

no wonder
No wonder the TV wasn't working. It wasn't plugged in.

the other day
Lee won the grand prize **the other day.** He's already bought a new car.

quite a few
I've asked those children **quite a few** times not to play football near my window. But they don't pay attention to me.

sooner or later
I know that Frank is always late, but **sooner or later** he'll get here.

take it easy
Take it easy. You don't have to drive so fast. We'll get there on time.

1. _____ recently, a short time ago

2. _____ not completely, but almost

3. _____ this one but not the next, then the next but not the one after that, and so on

4. _____ many

5. _____ don't worry, don't give it a thought

6. _____
_____ eventually, after some time

7. _____ calm down, relax, don't worry

8. _____ most important (reason)

9. _____ different from what you expected

10. _____ not surprising

Practice

A. Answer each question with **yes** or **no.** Explain your answer.

1. Sally calls her mother long distance on Sunday, but not every Sunday. She calls one Sunday but not the next; then she calls the Sunday after that, and so on. Does she call her mother every other Sunday?

2. Amy is a brilliant student, but whenever there's a test, she worries and spends hours and hours studying. Does she take it easy before a test?

3. After one week in bed with the flu, today I feel better. But I need a few more days to feel my best. Do I feel more or less okay?

4. Tyler got a very low grade on his composition because of his terrible grammar. Did he make a few mistakes?

5. I saw Barbara at the supermarket recently, but I can't remember when. Did I see her the other day?

6. If Jerry didn't call by now, he won't call. Will he call before long?

7. When we saw the big black clouds, we thought it would rain. But it didn't rain. Did it rain, after all?

8. The landlord is slow about making repairs, but he does make them. Does the landlord make repairs sooner or later?

9. Rick doesn't care about his family or friends. For him, money is the most important thing. Does Rick love money above all?

10. Jesse used to come to work late every day. He never did anything right. Is it correct to say no wonder he received a large raise?

11. Catherine offered to bring some food for the party, but Keith told her not to bring any because there would be enough. Did Keith tell her to never mind about bringing food?

B. Each example has the correct idiom, but there is one error with each idiom. Find the error and correct it.

1. There are quite a many tornadoes in our state each year.

2. Guess who I saw another day.

3. Look at the dark sky. I think it's going to rain after any.

4. Take it relax. This exercise is fun. Don't work so hard.

5. I'm more and less sure they'll vote for us.

6. Never mind, dad; I can fix the car.

7. Before all, remember to be polite when you meet them.

8. You go skiing and soon or later you fall down.

9. Never wonder you feel sick. You ate too much.

10. Try our banana-chocolate-raisin-nut ice cream sundae, and before longer you'll want another one!

11. We worked as a pair on the idioms exercise. Each of us did any other example.

Conversation

Practice each conversation with a partner.

SITUATION 1

Mike is very worried about his job interview tomorrow.

MIKE: I'm so worried I'm going to do the wrong thing.

JENNY: Just take it easy, Mike. I'm sure everything will be fine.

MIKE: I hope so.

JENNY: When you meet the boss, above all, look him in the eye, smile, and shake hands.

SITUATION 2

Ted and Laura enter their apartment on a hot summer day.

LAURA: It's really cold in here.

TED: No wonder it's so cold. The air conditioner was on high.

SITUATION 3

Frank and Mario are talking about the game.

FRANK: What do you think of the game so far?

MARIO: It's great! At first, I thought we'd lose for sure. But now I think we'll win after all.

On Your Own

Work with a partner. Choose three idioms. Write a short conversation for each idiom. Then act out your conversations.

Discussion

Work with a partner or in a small group. Do the following activities.

1. **Take it easy** and **never mind** are both intended to calm people down. What idioms do you have in your native language to calm people down?

2. **Before long** and **sooner or later** can both be used to describe situations in which people have to pay for the consequences of their actions. What stories or proverbs do you know where these idioms could be used?

3. We use **no wonder** when something suddenly becomes clear. Tell a story where you can use this idiom.

UNIT 20

Idioms with Words That Go Together II

Reading

Read the story. Then discuss the questions.

For a Change

No one is lucky all the time. But **once in a while,** something really good happens. **As a matter of fact,** something really good happened to me recently.

Each week my brother and I buy one lottery ticket. We **take turns.** One week he buys. The next week, I buy. This week it was different. **For a change,** my brother gave the money to his girlfriend, and she bought the ticket. He didn't see any problem. We never win. So he thought he **might as well** let her go buy the ticket. And we won forty-six million dollars and seven cents!

Now we have to share it three ways. Even so, I think we got a good deal.

1. When you do something **once in a while,** do you do it often?

2. When you **take turns** with someone doing something, how are the two of you working?

3. Why do people do things **for a change**? What would you like to do for a change?

Meanings

Each example has an idiom made up of words that go together. Read the example carefully to find the meaning of the idiom. Then look at the definitions below. Write the idiom next to its definition. **Note:** You will use the same definition for two idioms.

all of a sudden I was halfway to work, when **all of a sudden** I remembered that I'd left the water running in the bathtub. I turned around and went back home to turn it off.

as a matter of fact Jimmy loves motorcycles. **As a matter of fact,** he has three of them in his garage.

even so Lydia is good at math. **Even so,** she had trouble doing the last homework problem.

for a change We always have hamburgers on Thursdays. Let's have snails **for a change.**

for a start I had a really bad morning. **For a start,** my alarm clock didn't ring. And that was just the first in a series of disasters.

in fact Yes, I have lost weight. **In fact,** I've lost twenty-two pounds.

might as well If we can't think of anywhere to go on Saturday, we **might as well** stay home.

once in a while I don't see my old friends often these days. We see one another only **once in a while.**

on purpose Don't tell me that was an accident. You did that **on purpose.**

on the whole I sometimes have eggs for breakfast. But, **on the whole,** I try to avoid eating them.

to take turns Let's **take turns** washing the dishes. You do them this year, and I'll do them next year.

1. _____ not often

2. _____ in truth, really (often used to restate
   _____ something more exactly)

3. _____ first you do it, then someone else does it,
   then you, then the other person, and so
   on

4. _____ in order to do something different

5. _____ because there is nothing better

6. _____ although there is a reason why not

7. _____ beginning with the first of many reasons

8. _____ suddenly

9. _____ mostly but not always

10. _____ not by accident, by plan

Practice

A. Answer each question with **yes** or **no.** Explain your answer.

1. Dave likes to drink coffee during the day, but sometimes he'll drink tea. Does he drink coffee on the whole?

2. Rush and Tina drove to San Francisco from Los Angeles. Tina drove all the way because Rush was afraid to drive on the highway. Did they take turns driving?

3. Mom always bakes a cake for my birthday. This year she went to the bakery to get one. Did she buy one for a change?

4. When I was young, we used to go to the mountains on weekends, but we don't go anymore. Do we still go to the mountains once in a while?

5. Carl told us he ran a long distance this morning but that was all. Did he in fact say how far he ran?

6. Rick Lorenzo loves to collect antique cars. He has eleven of them. As a matter of fact, does Rick have eleven antique cars?

7. The man walking in front of me had thick brown hair. Then came a strong wind. When I looked at him a moment later, he had no hair. Did his hairpiece come off all of a sudden?

8. Donna promised to bring me a cup of coffee, but she accidentally spilled it on the way. Did she spill it on purpose?

9. We don't have enough time to finish cleaning the garage today. It's a good idea to stop and finish tomorrow morning. Is it true that we might as well finish tomorrow?

10. We should move from this apartment. First, we have to travel a long way to work. And that's just one reason. Is it true that, for a start, we should move because the apartment is too far from work?

11. Scott's father is very busy at work. But he coached the baseball team this year. Is it true that Scott's father is busy, but he made time to coach the team even so?

B. Each sentence has the correct idiom, but there is one error with each idiom. Find the error and correct it.

1. All a sudden it started to rain.

2. Arthur hurt his ankle as he was playing tennis. Even, that didn't stop him from winning the game.

3. I took a different route to school today for change.

4. We left the lights on in the house by purpose.

5. He's very tall. On fact, he is six feet, five inches.

6. It's getting late, and so we as well might go home.

7. We take turn doing the laundry.

8. There are a few things wrong with my new apartment. But, on a whole, I like it.

9. As a matter fact, it took three hours and twenty-one minutes to get here.

10. We usually watch television. Once in while we go to the movies.

11. Terry needs to get better grades. At a start, he should spend less time watching TV and more time studying.

Conversation

Practice each conversation with a partner.

SITUATION 1

A mother and daughter are at home.

LIN: May I go out with Maggie after dinner?

MOM: No, you may not. For a start, you haven't done your homework, and you haven't cleaned up your room.

LIN: As a matter of fact, Mom, I just finished my composition for my English class, made my bed, and put my clothes in the closet.

SITUATION 2

Two people who work together are talking.

TOM: Do you ever go hiking?

JERRY: Funny you should say that. Last Sunday, Beth and I decided to go hiking in the mountains near our house just for a change.

TOM: How was it?

JERRY: As a matter of fact, we both loved it, and we're going to go again this weekend.

SITUATION 3

Cam and Jean are at home.

CAM: Is there anything good on television?

JEAN: Nothing that you'd like.

CAM: Well, I might as well go to bed and read my book.

On Your Own

Work with a partner. Choose three idioms. Write a short conversation for each idiom. Then act out your conversations.

Discussion

Work with a partner or in a small group. Do the following activities.

1. **As a matter of fact** and **in fact** are both used before we say something more exactly. What words do you use in your native language before you say something exactly?

2. **For a start** begins the first of many reasons. Think of something that is necessary for you to do. Make a list of reasons why you should do it. Use **for a start** to begin your reasons.

3. When somebody does something **on purpose,** it is not an accident. He or she wanted to do it. Tell a story using this idiom.

Idioms Review

Review for Units 1–3

Circle the word or phrase that helps explain the meaning of the idiom in each sentence.

1. If an invitation arrives **out of the blue,** it's

   a. unexpected.

   b. for a wedding.

   c. from another country.

2. "She got **the green light** from her boss" means

   a. her boss said it was okay to go ahead.

   b. her boss told her to stop.

   c. her boss told her to hurry.

3. Someone who **goes bananas**

   a. goes shopping.

   b. goes crazy.

   c. gets fat.

4. If the final exam was **a piece of cake,** it was

   a. very difficult.

   b. very easy.

   c. too long.

5. If something is **second to none,** it's

   a. the worst.

   b. only second best.

   c. the best.

6. If you take **forty winks,** you

   a. have a short sleep.

   b. go out for lunch.

   c. go out for about an hour.

7. If you see something **in black and white,** it's

   a. typed.

   b. easy to understand.

   c. photocopied.

8. If you bought a **lemon,** it means you bought

   a. a yellow fruit.

   b. a great car.

   c. a machine that doesn't work.

9. If you're **of two minds** about something, you're

   a. very pleased.

   b. unsure.

   c. very sure.

10. If Laura's **in seventh heaven,** she's

   a. feeling very sick.

   b. very happy.

   c. unhappy.

11. If Anatoly's **green with envy,** he's

    a. new at something.

    b. happy.

    c. jealous.

12. If Yehudi's **in a pickle,** he's

    a. in trouble.

    b. in the hospital.

    c. in a good mood.

Review for Units 4–6

Circle the word or phrase that helps explain the meaning of the idiom in each sentence.

1. If Norman tells you to **shake a leg,** he wants you to

    a. jump higher.

    b. dance.

    c. hurry.

2. If something **costs an arm and a leg,** it's

    a. half-price.

    b. very expensive.

    c. on discount this month.

3. "It's the **real McCoy**" means it's

    a. the real thing.

    b. a good copy.

    c. a bad copy.

4. If you're **pulling Abigail's leg,** you're

   a. joking with her.

   b. hurting her.

   c. stopping her.

5. **A man of means** is

   a. poor.

   b. rich.

   c. educated.

6. If you **see eye to eye** with Miguel, you

   a. agree with him.

   b. hate him.

   c. miss him.

7. If Yoko is **chicken,** she's

   a. scared.

   b. crazy.

   c. poor.

8. Someone who **works like a dog**

   a. sleeps a lot.

   b. works hard.

   c. never works.

9. **A wise guy**

   a. is intelligent.

   b. always tells the truth.

   c. is a know-it-all.

10. If Leroy **talks turkey,** he

    a. tells jokes.

    b. says stupid things.

    c. talks directly.

11. **A bookworm** is someone who

    a. loves to read.

    b. hates books.

    c. destroys books.

12. Any **Tom, Dick, or Harry** is

    a. anyone whose name is Tom, Dick, or Harry.

    b. no one special, just anybody.

    c. the best person available for a job.

Review for Units 7–9

Circle the word or phrase that helps explain the meaning of the idiom in each sentence.

1. If you **put your cards on the table,** you

    a. aren't hiding anything.

    b. have no more money.

    c. stop working.

2. If something is **dirt cheap,** it's

    a. not cheap.

    b. not good.

    c. very cheap.

3. If a place is **spick-and-span,** it's

   a. old.

   b. very clean.

   c. dirty.

4. If Virgil tells a **cock-and-bull story,** he's telling

   a. an old story.

   b. lies.

   c. children's stories.

5. If Ntozake is **up the creek,** she's

   a. feeling great.

   b. in trouble.

   c. suddenly rich.

6. Someone who's **off base** is

   a. wrong.

   b. crazy

   c. unintelligent.

7. If Bernard's **over the hill,** he's

   a. still married.

   b. out of trouble.

   c. too old.

8. **"By and large"** means

   a. mostly.

   b. sometimes.

   c. never.

9. If something's **out of this world,** it's

   a. terrible.

   b. excellent.

   c. unlucky.

10. If you **get a kick out of something,** you

    a. hate it.

    b. enjoy it.

    c. are tired of it.

11. "We arrived **safe and sound**" means we

    a. arrived with no problems.

    b. had many problems.

    c. arrived late.

12. **A good sport**

    a. is good at sports.

    b. gets excited easily.

    c. doesn't complain.

Review for Units 10–12

Circle the word or phrase that explains the meaning of the idiom in each sentence.

1. Someone who **has a screw loose** is

   a. relaxed.

   b. worried.

   c. crazy.

2. **"To cough up"** means

   a. to pay.

   b. to die.

   c. to lie.

3. Someone who's **as sharp as a tack** is

   a. nervous.

   b. clever.

   c. angry.

4. **A fly in the ointment** is

   a. lucky.

   b. angry.

   c. a problem.

5. "John **threw in the towel**" means

   a. John was angry.

   b. John gave up.

   c. John finished showering.

6. Someone who's **bushed** is

   a. old.

   b. happy.

   c. exhausted.

7. Someone who **takes pains to do something**

   a. leaves it unfinished.

   b. doesn't do it well.

   c. takes the trouble to do it.

8. If Belinda **"beats around the bush,"** that means she

 a. leaves town.

 b. talks angrily.

 c. doesn't give a direct answer.

9. If Kyle **"gets burned,"** that means he gets

 a. cheated.

 b. killed.

 c. rejected.

10. **"A bed of roses"** means

 a. a comfortable, easy situation.

 b. difficult problems.

 c. a short time.

11. If Kostas is **a wet blanket,** he's

 a. very serious.

 b. always happy.

 c. always complaining.

12. **"In a nutshell"** means

 a. with great difficulty.

 b. in a few words.

 c. in a letter.

Review for Units 13–15

Circle the word or phrase that explains the meaning of the idiom in each sentence.

1. If something is **a breeze,** it's

    a. cold.

    b. difficult.

    c. easy.

2. **"Hot under the collar"** means

    a. sick.

    b. angry.

    c. happy.

3. **"In no time"** means

    a. never.

    b. quickly.

    c. very late.

4. If you **lose your shirt,** you lose

    a. your time.

    b. your job.

    c. everything.

5. When Liza **calls it a day,** she

    a. stops working.

    b. starts working.

    c. takes a short break.

6. **"On a shoestring"** means

   a. with almost no money.

   b. with almost no time.

   c. carefully.

7. If you do something **on the spur of the moment,** you do it

   a. too late.

   b. after a lot of thinking.

   c. immediately, without planning.

8. If Reiko **"breaks the ice,"** it means she

   a. begins a conversation with a stranger.

   b. has a bad temper.

   c. laughs a lot.

9. **"In the nick of time"** means

   a. at midnight.

   b. very early.

   c. just before it's too late.

10. **"It's raining cats and dogs"** means

    a. a short light rain.

    b. it's raining hard.

    c. it's not raining anymore.

11. If you **keep your shirt on,** you

    a. don't get upset.

    b. don't get sleepy.

    c. don't get undressed.

12. If Nadia is **under the weather,** she's

    a. in a bad mood.

    b. sick.

    c. feeling good.

Review for Units 16–18

Circle the word or phrase that explains the meaning of the idiom in each sentence.

1. If something's **on the house,** it's

    a. free.

    b. expensive.

    c. out of reach.

2. **"As fit as a fiddle"** means

    a. not healthy.

    b. very healthy.

    c. the right size.

3. "John **hit the ceiling**" means

    a. John scored a point.

    b. John became very angry.

    c. John was very sick.

4. If a place is **topsy-turvy,** it's

    a. big.

    b. neat

    c. disorganized.

5. If something is **as plain as day,** it's

   a. easy to understand.

   b. not clear.

   c. very boring.

6. Something **hush-hush** is

   a. strange.

   b. crunchy.

   c. secret.

7. If you're **"as hard as nails,"** it means you

   a. are busy.

   b. are dead.

   c. don't forgive.

8. **"Under the table"** means

   a. quickly.

   b. secretly.

   c. slowly.

9. **"As happy as a lark"** means

   a. noisy.

   b. never happy.

   c. very happy.

10. If Javier is **wishy-washy,** he's

    a. very clean.

    b. very undecided.

    c. very boring.

11. If you **drive** Boris **up the wall,** you

    a. make him crazy.

    b. win in an election.

    c. throw him out.

12. **"Humdrum"** means

    a. exciting.

    b. funny.

    c. routine.

Review for Units 19–20

Circle the word or phrase that explains the meaning of the idiom in each sentence.

1. **"Quite a few"** means

   a. none.

   b. a few.

   c. many.

2. **"Above all"** means

   a. different.

   b. most important.

   c. suddenly.

3. If you do something **on purpose,** you

   a. do it because you want to.

   b. do it by accident.

   c. do it for your school.

4. **"The other day"** means

   a. yesterday.

   b. tomorrow.

   c. recently.

5. **"All of a sudden"** means

   a. exactly.

   b. suddenly.

   c. in a few minutes.

6. **"Sooner or later"** means

   a. eventually.

   b. in the past.

   c. never.

7. **"Once in a while"** means

   a. once in the past.

   b. usually.

   c. not often.

8. When you say **"in fact,"** you mean

   a. in place of something.

   b. truly.

   c. in short.

Glossary of Idioms

The number in parentheses after each idiom is the unit in which the idiom is introduced.

above all (19) most important (reason)

after all (19) different from what you expected

all of a sudden (20) suddenly

apple of one's eye, the (2) someone's favorite person, a well-loved person

as a matter of fact (20) in truth, really (often used to restate something more exactly)

as blind as a bat (6) not able to see well because of very bad eyesight

as busy as a bee (17) very busy

as fit as a fiddle (17) very healthy

as good as gold (17) very good, well-behaved

as happy as a lark (17) very happy

as hard as nails (17) very hard and cold, not forgiving

as hungry as a bear (17) very hungry

as plain as day (17) very easy to see or understand

as quiet as a mouse (6) making almost no noise, being shy and not talking much

as regular as clockwork (17) always at the same time

as sharp as a tack (10) clever, intelligent

as sick as a dog (17) very unwell

as stubborn as a mule (17) not willing to change one's mind, very set in one's ideas

as weak as a kitten (17) not very strong

at first sight (3) after a quick look, before really thinking about one's feeling about something

back and forth (9) from one place to another and back to the first place

baloney (2) nonsense

bark up the wrong tree, to (12) to make the wrong choice and waste one's efforts

beat around the bush, to (12) to waste time by not giving a direct answer

bed of roses, a (12) a comfortable, easy situation

before long (19) eventually, after some time

be in someone else's shoes, to (13) to be in someone else's place

big mouth, a (4) a person who talks too much and does not keep secrets

big time, the (14) a high level of success

bitter pill to swallow, a (11) something difficult and unpleasant to experience

black market, the (1) the market not controlled by the government, where things are sold in private and often against the law

blood is thicker than water (11) relatives are the most important people

bookworm, a (6) someone who reads a lot

break the ice, to (15) to begin a conversation with a stranger

breeze, a (15) something easy for a person to do

bring down the house, to (16) to make an audience clap and laugh enthusiastically

bury the hatchet, to (10) to agree to no longer be enemies

bushed (12) very tired, exhausted

by and large (9) mostly, most often

by heart (4) by memory

call it a day, to (14) to stop doing something

chicken (6) afraid, scared

cock-and-bull story, a (9) an untrue story

come rain or shine (15) no matter how hard it is to do

copycat, a (6) a person who wants to do the same thing as other people

cost an arm and a leg, to (4) to be very expensive

cough up, to (11) to pay money

cream someone, to (2) to totally beat someone in a game

dillydally, to (18) to hesitate, to waste time by moving slowly

dirt cheap (7) very inexpensive

down the drain (16) wasted, lost

down-to-earth (7) honest and direct, sensible and practical

dressed to kill (13) in one's best clothes and looking good

drive someone up the wall, to (16) to make someone angry or crazy

early bird, an (6) the first person to be somewhere, a person who gets out of bed early

eat like a horse, to (6) to eat a lot

even so (20) although there is a reason why not

every other (19) this one but not the next, then the next but not the one after that, and so on

fair and square (9) honestly, without cheating

fair-weather friend, a (15) a person who doesn't help when a friend is in trouble

feather in one's cap, a (13) something to be proud of and to feel good about

feel blue, to (1) to feel sad

feel it in one's bones, to (11) to know something, often before seeing it or before it happens

fishy (2) suspicious, not right or honest

flash in the pan, a (10) something that starts out well but that may not continue

fly in the ointment, a (11) a problem

for a change (20) in order to do something different

for a start (20) beginning with the first of many reasons

for the time being (14) temporarily, just for the present moment

forty winks (3) a short sleep, a nap

fuddy-duddy (18) someone who doesn't like change

full of hot air (15) talking a lot but never doing what one says

get a kick out of something, to (8) to enjoy something a lot

get burned, to (11) to have a bad experience, to be cheated

get one's foot in the door, to (16) to take the first steps to start something, to get an opening

give someone a taste of his/her own medicine, to (11) to do something bad to someone after the other person has done the same bad thing

go bananas, to (2) to go crazy

go downhill, to (7) to go down in numbers or in quality, to get worse

go Dutch, to (5) to share the cost, to pay one's own bill

go fly a kite, to (8) to go away or stop annoying someone, usually said in anger

good sport, a (8) someone who does not complain if he or she loses or who does not boast if he or she wins

green light, the (1) the okay to start something

green with envy (1) jealous of someone else's good fortune

handle someone with kid gloves, to (13) to be careful not to anger someone

have a lot of nerve, to (11) to act so badly and impolitely that it actually takes courage to do so

have a screw loose, to (10) to be crazy

have a sweet tooth, to (4) to like sweet foods very much

have one's head in the clouds, to (15) not to know or understand what is going on

head over heels in love (4) very much in love

high time (14) almost too late to do something

hit home, to (16) to make someone really realize something

hit the ceiling, to (16) to suddenly become very angry

hit the hay, to (12) to go to bed and sleep

hold one's breath, to (11) to pause, to stop and think

hotshot (18) someone who is very good at something but who often isn't very modest

hot under the collar (13) angry

humdrum (18) routine, repeated activities

hush-hush (18) secret

in a nutshell (12) in a few words

in a pickle (2) in trouble

in black and white (1) very clear and easy to understand

in fact (20) in truth, really (often used to restate something more exactly)

in no time (14) quickly

in seventh heaven (3) extremely happy

in the black (1) having money

in the nick of time (14) just before it is too late

in the red (1) owing money, in debt

in the same boat (8) in the same situation

ins and outs (9) all the details

jack of all trades, a (5) a person who can do many things

keep it under one's hat, to (13) to keep something secret

keep one's shirt on, to (13) not to get angry, to be patient

keep the ball rolling, to (8) to make something continue to happen

keep up with the Joneses, to (5) to want the same nice things that other people have

kill time, to (14) to waste time waiting for something else to happen

last straw, the (12) the final thing after a series of bad things, the thing that finally makes one angry

lemon, a (2) something that does not work, usually an electrical appliance or mechanical item

long face, a (4) a sad, dissatisfied expression

lose one's shirt, to (13) to lose a lot of money

make a mountain out of a molehill, to (7) to make a big problem out of a small problem

make time, to (14) to do something although you did not plan it and you are already busy

man/girl Friday, a (5) someone who does a large variety of tasks on the job

man/woman of means, a (5) a rich person

might as well (20) because there is nothing better

more or less (19) not completely, but almost

mumbo jumbo (18) language that cannot easily be understood, jargon

never mind (19) don't worry, don't give it a thought

nip something in the bud, to (12) to stop something when it's just beginning

no dice (8) no, a negative answer

nosey (4) always wanting to know other people's business and what other people are doing

no wonder (19) not surprising

nuts (2) very crazy, very upset

odds and ends (9) a variety of small items, the pieces left over

off base (8) not correct, inappropriate

of two minds (3) having trouble making a decision about something

on a shoestring (13) with very little money

on cloud nine (3) extremely happy

on pins and needles (10) very nervous and anxious

on purpose (20) not by accident, by plan

on second thought (3) changing one's mind after thinking more about something

on the ball (8) very good at doing things, effective and efficient

on the fence (16) undecided

on the house (16) free, for nothing

on the shelf (16) too old, no longer of use

on the spur of the moment (14) immediately, without planning

on the whole (20) mostly but not always

once in a blue moon (7) almost never, very seldom

once in a while (20) not often

other day, the (19) recently, a short time ago

out of the blue (1) by surprise, unexpectedly

out of the woods (7) out of the trouble or difficulty

out of this world (7) excellent, very good

over the hill (7) getting too old

pain in the neck, a (4) something or someone that annoys or bothers a person

pan out, to (10) to succeed, to have a good result

peach, a (2) a very nice person

peanuts (2) a very small amount of money

piece of cake, a (2) something that is very easy to do

pigheaded (6) not taking advice, stubborn

pitter-patter (18) sound of quick, light taps, like the sound of rain or children's feet

potluck (10) a meal in which everybody brings a food to eat

pull someone's leg, to (4) to joke, to kid or trick someone

put one's cards on the table, to (8) not to hide anything, to explain the situation fully and honestly

put two and two together, to (3) to finally understand something, to come to a conclusion

quite a few (19) many

rain cats and dogs, to (15) to rain very hard

real McCoy, the (5) a true example of something

red carpet, the (1) special honors for a special or important person

red tape (1) complicated official procedures and forms

right and left (9) in large numbers, from every side

right off the bat (8) immediately, without delay

run in the family, to (5) to be characterized by something common to many members of a family

safe and sound (9) with no damage or injury

save something for a rainy day, to (15) to prepare for trouble, usually by saving money

second nature (3) easy and natural to someone

second to none (3) the very best

see eye to eye, to (4) to agree completely

shake a leg, to (4) to hurry up, move faster

sick and tired (11) very annoyed, very tired of doing something

sink or swim (8) fail or succeed, no matter what

six of one, half a dozen of the other (3) no difference, either choice okay

sixth sense (3) a special feeling for something, or a special understanding of things

smart aleck, a (5) someone who acts as if he or she knows everything and is often rude about it

smell a rat, to (6) to think there may be something wrong

snowed under (15) having a lot of work to do

soap opera (10) a drama on TV or radio that continues over time and in which the characters have many problems

song and dance, a (9) a long explanation, a long excuse that is often not true

sooner or later (19) eventually, after some time

spick-and-span (9) very clean

sponge off, to (10) to take money or hospitality and never pay anything back

stuffed shirt, a (13) someone who lives by the rules and is very formal

take it easy (19) calm down, relax, don't worry

take one's time, to (14) not to hurry

take pains, to (11) to take a lot of trouble to do something

take steps, to (16) to do something

take turns, to (20) first you do it, then someone else does it, then you, then the other person, and so on

talk turkey, to (6) to talk openly and directly

through the grapevine (12) from what one person said to another, by rumor

throw in the towel, to (10) to accept defeat or loss

tied to someone's apron strings (13) always following a stronger person

time is right, the (14) it is a good time to do something

tip of the iceberg, the (7) small part of a larger problem

tip-top (18) best

Tom, Dick, or Harry (5) nobody special, just any person

topsy-turvy (18) not organized, messy

turn over a new leaf, to (12) to start over again, to start a new and better life

under the table (16) secretly, usually doing something against the law

under the weather (15) sick

up a tree (12) in a difficult situation from which you cannot find a way out

up the creek (7) in trouble

wear and tear (9) damage that happens as something gets old and used

weather the storm, to (15) to wait and be patient until things get better

wet blanket, a (10) a person who doesn't enjoy things and keeps others from enjoying them

wheeler-dealer, a (18) a person who is always making business deals and trying to get the best deal

white lie, a (1) something that is not true but that causes no harm

win by a landslide, to (7) to get almost all of the votes

wise guy, a (5) someone who acts as if he or she knows everything and is often rude about it

wishy-washy (18) undecided, weak, not definite and clear

work like a dog, to (6) to work very hard